The Ultimate Tip

Roanoke, VA
moonlitediting.com

The Ultimate Tip
A Beginner's Guide to Waiting Tables

Dexter Hall

© 2013, 2019

Contents

Chapter One:
The Ultimate Job Security 1

Chapter Two:
Getting Started (for Food Service Virgins) 11

Chapter Three:
Making Allies — Beating the System from Within 19

Chapter Four:
Your Appearance 41

Chapter Five:
Crew Bonding 47

Chapter Six:
The Basics 51

Chapter Seven:
Food and Wine Knowledge 73

Chapter Eight:
The Six Magic Words 81

Chapter Nine:
Losing It 89

Chapter Ten:
Safety First 95

Chapter Eleven:
The Joy of Side Work 103

Chapter Twelve:
Don't Make Honey Where You Make Your Money 107

Chapter Thirteen:
The Weeds 113

Chapter Fourteen:
Restaurant Pranks 119

Chapter Fifteen:
The Dark Side of Waiting Tables 129

Chapter Sixteen:
The Ultimate Tip 135

Glossary of Restaurant Terminology 139

Chapter One:
The Ultimate Job Security

I started my career in the great food service army when I was only eighteen. It was the mid-eighties, and I worked in a fast-food restaurant. The restaurant chain had just started to sell salads as well as burgers. I worked the drive-thru window, where I was forced to wear a painter's cap that read, "LET ME TOSS YOUR SALAD." True story.

The point is, no one ever says growing up, "Oh, gee, instead of being an astronaut or a princess, what I really, really, want to do when I grow up is wait on tables in a restaurant," any more than someone wants to grow up working in a dry cleaner's or a dirty factory. In a restaurant, it's demeaning, degrading, and sometimes, you don't get paid at all for your hard work. So why would anyone end up doing it in the first place? I don't know.

People come to the restaurant world for many reasons, but very few come because they wish to serve ungrateful human beings. Maybe you came because you just gotta make some quick cash right now . . . maybe 'cause you're so behind on the bills, or you just flat-out need some cash to get you through so that you don't have to move back home and deal with people who thought you couldn't make it. Or maybe just because you're desperate for personal reasons (that you really don't have to share).

Whatever the reasons that have forced you to work as a modern-day slave to people who go out to eat and drink, I would like to say just one word: Welcome. If anyone in your past has been a jerk to you and said you'd never make it on your own, they're lying—probably just to keep you down. The point is that you can make it—no, scratch that. You are *most definitely* going to make it.

Welcome.

Chances are if you're reading this guide right now, someone has told you about it. I'm glad. Working in the food service industry is hard—very hard. But what isn't? And besides, you already know that. What I want to do is make sure that after you read this, you make every extra penny possible, every time.

The Ultimate Tip is the maximum amount of gratuity a guest will leave because their server has exceeded all expectations. Every server needs to strive to make the ultimate tip from every table he or she waits on. And I can show you how. God knows I wish someone had told me all the things I'm about to tell you when I first started out.

The point of this whole manual is that there's no one quick way to double the amount of tips you're currently getting. However, based on my last twenty-five years' experience in the food service industry, I know that if you use all the information I give you, you'll make a hell of a lot more money than you are right now.

I will teach you how to upgrade your skill level, or increase your stress load capacity, or get you working in a more expensive restaurant. It's really not that hard, even though many successful people today would tell you that working in a restaurant was the most challenging job they ever had. Still interested?

Let me tell you how I started out . . .

From meager beginnings

That fast-food joint back when I was eighteen was the only job I could get that didn't require any experience. The pay was sucky, and the customers were even worse. I tried my best to do my job correctly, but every day, I would get stressed out and feel like a loser. Day by day, I learned new skills — especially how to deal with customers — and things got a little better. Just a little.

I tried college for a while, and — surprise, surprise — didn't graduate. What I did do while I was there was work in the student cafeteria serving more than a thousand people per meal during the school session, as well as a professional football team that trained there in the summer.

After that, I got a job at a hotel restaurant that fluctuated from being crazy busy to excruciatingly dead. One night we would have twenty customers, and the next night, when there was a convention booked, we would do more than three hundred dinners. My server skills then were so weak, I could barely open a bottle of wine while holding it between my knees.

Then more stuff happened, and I ended up working at one of those national franchise chain restaurants that sells lots of appetizers and offers coupons. The one I worked at was actually the corporation's flagship store and did more volume than any other franchise they had. I lasted there for a couple of years but was still gaining restaurant expertise.

I then worked in some pretty fancy private boutique restaurants for a while and loved it. I had enough skill, talent, and youth to quickly outsell the veteran servers on the staff. I kept traveling around, though, never satisfied. I worked in an expensive, Cajun-seafood-themed restaurant for a while, as well as a couple of pricey American bistros.

Next, I worked for four years in one of the country's most exclusive four-star steakhouse chain restaurants. On special days of the year, we had more celebrities dining with us than regular folks.

I peaked out at a five-star restaurant on the East Coast that was the most expensive restaurant in a city filled with expensive places to eat. Sometimes, I even got checked out by secret service because of the important people I was waiting on. By this time, my skill set was so advanced that in pre-shift nightly service meetings, I would be assigned to take on any returning guests who had a history of complaining, because my boss knew I wouldn't give them a chance to complain about anything. Also, whenever food critics or travel writers were spotted within the establishment, I would be instantly assigned to wait on them so they would get the best possible experience.

I was that good. I still am. Somewhere in America right now, I'm still wowing my guests with the best service they've ever received. I should know how to do it by now . . . I've been doing it for twenty-five years! And it pays a helluva lot better than handing out fries through a drive-thru window—tossed salad or not.

These days, wherever I'm working, my bosses always insist that I train all the new hires. It takes some time and is not always easy. Some people just don't have it; some do. I'm pretty sure that most people who met me back when I was a brand-new server would've placed me in the "don't have it" category. God knows I certainly fucked up enough meals to prove them right. Oh God, I ruined more customers' meals through inexperience than I will ever own up to. But eventually, I got better. You can, too.

I have literally trained hundreds, if not thousands, of people in the art of serving. I lost count at some point. To this day, a person will sometimes come up to me on the street, hug me, and tell me all about the positive experiences that resulted from my training—as well as the life lessons it taught them. Naturally, I try to be polite and act as if I actually remember them. Sometimes I do, but most of the time, it's all a blur.

I've been doing this for a long, long time. I still love doing it, though—in the right restaurant, and serving the right guests. You see, I have a passion to exceed guests' expectations and "wow" them every time. The other thing that excites me is when I can educate somebody new and show them the ropes. I love watching a rookie server make his first huge tip.

When I can actually talk to a restaurant "virgin" and show them the ends and outs, it feels good to me because I know that for once, I'm not just working for a tip—I'm empowering somebody else. I'm going to help them make more money for college, baby formula, their rent, or whatever.

I am told that in every profession, the veterans always jealously guard what they know from the new kids so as not to be threatened by them. Go figure. To serve in a restaurant, you have to be attentive, responsive, knowledgeable, and quick—*especially* quick. Hey, I'm almost forty-five now, and there's only so much longer I can do this before my knees, eyes, or liver give out.

I want to give you the crash course I wish somebody would've taken the time to give to me. I want to let you know what it's like to work in a restaurant before you even decide to do it. Or, if you're already suffering in the great food and beverage army, I want to make damn sure you're making every penny possible.

Every restaurant is different, just like each snowflake is unique. However, even between differently shaped snowflakes, I think there are more similarities than differences. Every snowflake is cold, white, and lacey. Every restaurant is competitive, demanding, and unfair. The first two parts, competitive and demanding, I can help you with. As far as the unfairness of it all, well, I can't change that fact. On the other hand, you can use the unfairness; it can either be unfair *against* a server, or unfair *in favor* of a talented and skilled one.

In every restaurant, customers come in with limited amounts of time and money to spend. In every restaurant, there are servers with different levels of skill who wait upon them. You can make twice as much money as the less skilled servers. I will teach you the best, smartest, and most profitable ways to double what you're making right now.

When a new server starts at a restaurant, the veteran servers are the ones who train them. Usually, they'll teach you just enough to get by without making mistakes. However, it's not always in their best interest to teach you everything they know. After all, they're competing with you to get the best sections and make the most money. They hold back a little knowledge and wisdom for themselves so they can easily outshine you.

But I'm not going to do that. I'm going to teach you every insight and trick I've learned in my twenty-five years' experience on the front lines of food service. It's not like I have to compete with you, after all. It's in my best interest to impress you with priceless knowledge so that you'll tell other servers how much this book helped you. Deal?

A nothing job?

First things first: Why should you even take a job in a restaurant if I'm over here making it sound so challenging? Well, come on—everybody already knows that the main reason many people take a job in a restaurant is that they're already desperate or can't hold down a "real" job. Most people who have nine-to-five jobs look at food and beverage jobs like a cautionary tale. They say things like, "Make sure you study hard, or you'll be waiting tables when you're thirty!" Well, I can tell you this much, gentle readers: Everybody thinks waiting tables is a piece of cake, that any monkey could do it.

But when the stock markets tanked, and the economy crashed, I was working at a four-star seafood restaurant in Baltimore, Maryland. Every day, all kinds of applications would come in from doctors, executives, and even stockbrokers. They were desperate for any kind of job that might bring them in even one hundred extra dollars a week. Doubtless, they were sure that because of their "higher education," they would be the first ones hired. After all, anybody could do this job, right? So, of course, they'd be the first ones picked.

Oh yes, they had degrees from colleges and universities, no doubt with years of student loans to pay off, but they had no clue how to deal with flesh-and-blood customers in a demanding economy. They didn't even know how to carry a tray of drinks, or how to ring in a food order correctly. My bosses never even called them back.

If you learn how to wait on tables correctly, my friends, you will have ultimate job security. No matter what happens in the world of global finance, if you have the skills to wait on tables, you can get a job in almost any restaurant on the spot. Every restaurant is always looking for a talented server. I'll show you how to be the best.

Chapter Two:

Getting Started

(For Food Service Virgins)

Okay—so let's figure out where to start off with you. Have you ever worked in a restaurant before? If the answer is no, then you're going to have to start off at the bottom of the food chain. I recommend that you get a job in a fast-food restaurant for a minimum of three months. That will give you the baseline experience of dealing with customers, ringing in orders, making change, dealing with stress, and coping with management. It is going to suck, but just remember that you are learning valuable things.

Next, apply at a cheap restaurant where servers get tips, like all-night breakfast restaurants or lunch diners. Work there for at least three months. You'll learn how to serve food correctly and how to turn tables efficiently for maximum tips.

Next, step it up a little. Apply at restaurants that serve alcohol, where the check average is going to be even higher. This will give you a basic working knowledge of beer, wine, and liquors. This will also give you important exposure to more demanding guests who will tip you even more when you satisfy them completely. Work there for another six months or so, and you will be able to apply at nicer restaurants and make even more money. Once you have accomplished this, you'll be able to correctly pick which restaurant you want to work for. Which brings me to a very important point:

PICK YOUR RESTAURANT MORE CAREFULLY THAN YOU WOULD CHOOSE YOUR LOVER.

(Because you can always find another lover, but a bitch gotta get paid.)

So . . .

Step 1: Choose your restaurant wisely.

Why should this even matter? After all, every restaurant serves food, right? That's where you're wrong, my babies. Just like assholes go to a cheap trailer park to beat their girlfriends, cheap assholes go to cheap restaurants to beat on their servers. The more expensive the place you work, the fewer wife-beaters you're going to see. Work in a place that's expensive enough to out-intimidate all the rednecks and cheapskates from ever encountering you in the first place.

Since you're going to be tipped based on the total amount of the check, that obviously means the higher the bill, the larger the gratuity you're likely to receive. Think fine dining — white linen tablecloths and candles are a sure giveaway. Look at each restaurant's menu; the average entree price should be at least twenty-five dollars.

See if they have a wine list. If they do not, don't even bother applying. If they do have a wine list, they should not sell bottles for less than twenty bucks and should have at least a few priced at one hundred and higher. Also, while you're snooping around your prospective restaurant, pay close attention to the staff's facial expressions. Do they seem happy? Do they look worried or nervous or stressed out of their minds?

Step 2: Assess the quality of the management.

If the staff seems oppressed, it's a sure sign of tyrannical management. See if you can identify the manager without him or her knowing. Observe how he speaks to his staff. Is he professional and polite, or irate and demeaning? Does her body language look threatening or welcoming? You definitely do *not* want to work in a hostile environment—unless there is a shit ton of cash to be made. The ideal manager interacts with her staff without making them feel nervous or scared.

Step 3: Pick which shift to work.

Choosing the restaurant where you will be employed helps determine how much money you'll make more than most factors. But also important is whether you work breakfast, lunch, or dinner.

For example, a server doing five double shifts at a diner is never going to make as much money as a fine dining server who works five single dinner shifts. So consider the shifts you want to work. Pretty much, the money you make from ten breakfast tickets is equal to five lunch tickets, which is equal to two dinner tickets. Translation: Dinnertime is where the money is! That's when the high-rollers come out to wine and dine and blow big money to impress each other.

Step 4: Apply for the job and nail the interview.

Believe it or not, even knowing what time to come inside a restaurant and ask for an application can make or break you. You, the prospective employee, need to know when it's the best time to show your face for the first time. Don't come in when the restaurant is at its busiest. See if you can come in an hour before they open, as the door will usually be unlocked for the employees to get inside and open up the place. Smile at the first person you see, and then ask them if you can fill out an application. Some restaurants will want you to fill it out on premises, and some will want you to take it with you and bring it back later. These days, some places will only let you complete an application online.

When you fill out the application, don't lie or make up any false work information. That kind of thing will only bite you in the ass later. Just be sure to put in there somewhere that you're a hard worker who is punctual and responsible. Make sure to have a phone number (one that's in service) so the manager can call you back to set up an interview.

When it's time to show up for the interview, be ready. Chances are, the manager who's going to interview you is already overworked, hung over, pissed off, and looking to find any reason not to like you. Show up sober, clean, and with restaurant-type clothes already on. This is not the time to flaunt your personal style. The restaurant manager is only trying to decide if you're smart and malleable enough to fit in with the pre-existing crew.

Simply tell him or her that you're a fast learner, a team player, punctual, and that you get along well with others—and don't talk too much. When a manager is thinking about hiring you, he's also thinking about how much he is going to have to deal with your shit. Minimize it. There will be plenty of time for him to regret his decision later.

At the conclusion of the interview, thank the manager for her time and verbally ask her for the job. Say something like, "I can tell this is a really exciting place to work, and I would like to be hired." Then, you'll just have to play the waiting game to see if you get the job. Usually, you will know for sure one way or another within a week.

Feel free to apply to as many restaurants as you like—it never hurts to have options. Eventually, some restaurant will be desperate enough to hire you, and then it will be time for . . .

Your first day on the job

If you have somehow managed to get yourself hired at a restaurant—God help you—it's time for your first day on the job.

The first day of employment in a restaurant is one of the most important ones. This is when management and your co-workers will size you up; the impression you make is likely to last quite a while, so don't screw it up.

Whatever time they want you to arrive, be ten minutes early. Find out ahead of time how to get there and where to park so you won't be late. Make sure you know what clothes to wear for your uniform and what supplies or waiter tools you're required to have. Most restaurants want you to bring at least three pens, something to write on, a lighter, and a wine opener or corkscrew.

Don't go out partying the night before, either. Take a sleeping pill or whatever you need to do to get to bed at a reasonable time so that you can show up well-rested and completely groomed.

There should be nothing about your appearance that is sloppy in any way. That said, your attitude is what matters most of all. Be ready to work, and work hard. Try to limit how many questions you ask. You'll likely be paired up with a senior member of the wait staff for training. Pay attention to every word he or she says.

Even if you're naturally talkative and outgoing, this is not the time to be chatty. Fly under the radar as much as possible for the first couple of days. No one in your new restaurant really gives a damn how much of a winning personality you have—at least, not at first. They just want to see how fast you can receive programming. Resistance is futile; you will be assimilated.

During each shift, stay busy and don't just stand around like you don't know what to do—especially if you don't know what to do. Find something, anything, no matter how menial, to keep your hands busy. Polish glassware, sweep the floor, sort the silverware, clean the bathrooms. Rest assured that while you're being trained, management is constantly watching you to see if you really are a hard worker or not.

When you finish your first shift, thank your trainer for showing you the ropes, as well as anyone else who helped you. Take home any reading material you've been given, like an employee handbook or menu guide. That night, study it as if your life depends on it, because your job definitely does. Use whatever memory tricks you have to quickly learn everything about your restaurant's menu and policies and bring you up to speed. That way, you will be waiting on tables and making tips as soon as possible.

There are always some employees who will see you, a new hire, as a threat. You can't do anything about that. What you can do, however, is make them feel like you're not out for their job. The best way to do this is to show up on time and defer to their judgment when they tell you something. Eventually, if you're any good at all, management will notice, and these so-called veteran servers' opinions of you won't matter at all. If you can manage this, then you're ready to make some allies.

Chapter Three:
Making Allies—Beating the System from Within

You gotta learn how to beat the system in a restaurant by making allies within the restaurant. You've got to learn how to do favors for everybody in every department so that you can call on them in when your ass is in deep trouble

Therefore, to make the maximum amount of money possible, you as a server must have a complete well-oiled team to rely upon. I know you might think that to make the largest tips, all you have to do is make the customers like you. This is only partly true. To really make some cash in a restaurant, *everyone* has to like you. And to accomplish this, you have to work the system. A server must have at least one ally in each of these departments of the restaurant:

- The front door/host stand
- Server assistant
- Bartender
- Cook, chef, back of the house
- Manager
- Dishwasher—yes, even the lowly dishwasher can screw you over if you betray his trust!

Even if you've found a good restaurant to work at, you will never maximize your earnings until you learn to beat the system.

The system says to show up on time, be ready to work, and wait for good customers to come and sit down in your section. Whether or not that last part happens, you will need more than mere luck to make the best money. You'll need at least one ally at the host stand.

Dealing with the host stand

It's easy for a frenzied server to look over to the host stand and think the hosts have the easiest job in the restaurant. They look all composed and calm and smiling. All they have to do, you think, is walk the guests into the restaurant, sit them down at a table, and hand them menus.

Nothing could be further from the truth. Whether the host stand is manned by hourly employees or by trained management staff, this is where the battle plan for each night is decided—long before service actually begins.

This is the war room, where a tight roster is carefully calculated. A skilled host looks at the total reservations for each night, where large parties should go, where VIPs want to be, as well as deciding how much leeway the restaurant has for walk-in business. They also decide which servers can take the most tables without generating complaints.

This is where the distribution of wealth is determined. The direction of the night's earnings—whose pockets that money ends up in—will be decided at the door. Will your section be filled with cheap complainers or wealthy, generous guests? The question is answered at the host stand. Try to see what the reservation schedule is for the night so that you can be prepared.

If you see that you have more than one table sitting down in your section at the same time, make an action plan for how to handle it. If you're on good terms with the host, you can ask him or her to switch one reservation for another so that you won't have two tables at once — a problem called getting "double-seated."

Every veteran in the restaurant industry dreads this. When you're double-seated, you have to decide which table to start with and which table to make wait. If you do get double-seated, try to find a coworker who can at least greet the other table and take drink orders while you're dealing with the first one. And how do you choose which one's first? Always pick the one that looks wealthier. They're likely to order bigger and tip better.

However, to get those good customers into your section in the first place, you have to win over the host stand. And in order to get the hosts to like you, you have to help them. Ask if they need assistance in any way, like: "Do you need me to bring you more menus," or "Would it help if I answered the phone sometimes," or "Do you need help with the coat check?" If the host likes you, he or she is far more likely to put more money in your pocket. On the flip side, pissing hosts off is sheer financial suicide.

Don't ever ask them to give you the best tables, either. Most hosts already think of waiters as being demanding and greedy and wanting all the money for themselves. Also, don't try to bribe the host stand with cash to get the best tables. Eventually, the other servers always find out and will take revenge in any way they can.

Be sure to always thank the host stand at the end of each shift by saying something like, "I know we were really booked tonight, but you kept everything running so smoothly," or "Thanks for spacing out my tables evenly so I didn't get double- or triple-seated. I really appreciate it!" In most restaurants, management pre-decides how and where the reserved tables will be distributed, but it's usually up to the host to choose where the walk-in tables will go.

When guests are leaving, the host will ask them, "How was everything tonight?" Hopefully, your guests will have had a positive experience and will say so. If you were a crappy server, they will bitch out the host stand. The result: the host won't want to seat you good tables in the future.

You're probably seeing how important the server-host relationship is. Here's another tip: Do *not* "hang out" at the host stand and chat. There are several good reasons to never do this:

- It looks unprofessional
- It detracts the host from doing his or her duties
- It keeps you out of your own section, where you should be selling and making that money

Never attempt to seat a group in your section that was supposed to go elsewhere. This is known as "table-stealing" and will cause you to be despised by your fellow servers.

A gentleman I used to wait on sometimes in Louisville, Kentucky, would tip his server a thousand dollars *every single time*; the stampede to seat him was ridiculous and hilarious. He was a rich redneck who would spend the day on the golf course getting drunk with his buddies.

Afterward, they'd grab some Hooters girls and come into our restaurant. He always bought our most expensive bottle of wine (Petrus, which cost a grand a bottle).

We usually tried to seat him outside on our patio, as he was quite loud and boisterous. I guess he felt entitled to be annoying because he spent so much money there and tipped so lavishly. One evening, one of his Hooters girls got up to use the bathroom and walked through an open sliding-glass door. While she was gone, however, someone had closed the glass door; upon her return, she didn't notice the door had been closed and totally face-planted into it.

The guys at her table, instead of being concerned, all laughed at her and said, "What a dumb bitch!" She went right up to "Mr. X," grabbed his glass of thousand-dollar-a-bottle wine, and threw it all over him. As it began dripping down his face and onto his golf shirt, I started laughing.

He turned to me and snarled, "What's so funny, Dexter?!"

"Man!" I said, "That's something you don't get to see every day!"

"What's that?" he demanded.

"A two-hundred-dollar stain on a twenty-dollar shirt," I told him. "Don't clean it, wring it!" The whole table then started laughing with me, and finally, he joined in. Luckily, he could take a joke, and yes, he did tip me a thousand dollars that night. Good times.

Another way to get on the hosts' good side is to bring them stuff. Oftentimes, they aren't allowed to leave the host stand, and they can get thirsty and hungry just like anybody else. If you can sneak them a Coke or a piece of bread hidden in a napkin, you can gain a powerful ally.

You can also offer to "watch the door" while they dash off for a quick bathroom break. They're only human, after all, and we all come equipped with a bladder. They won't forget this kindness when it comes time to decide where to put the good tables later on.

If you don't like how a host seated you, never bitch about it behind their back. Everyone in a restaurant gossips, and it will get back to them. If you feel like you must talk with the host, resolve it at the end of the night when all the stress has dissipated. Do it one-on-one so that no one else hears, or else the host will be embarrassed or pissed off. Remember, the host holds the keys to the kingdom! The money is decided at the door. Without their goodwill towards you, you might as well hang it up.

I know it might not sound like much, but it can be a real game-changer if the host feels like you're on his or her side. If you've done this much, then it's time to find an assistant.

Allying yourself with the bussers

The server assistant, back-server, busser—whatever you call this coworker, even though she may seem like the lowliest person in the front-of-the-house hierarchy, she's probably the most important factor in how smoothly your shift goes. Your server assistant is the Robin to your Batman, the yin to your yang, and the wind beneath your wings, all in one!

Here's why: Not only does the server assistant work like a red blood cell in the body, distributing nutrients and liquids while removing wastes, he's also an extra set of eyes and ears on your guests.

Often, guests will say things to a busboy in a more relaxed way than they will when talking with their fine dining server (when they're trying to be all formal and suave). Or your assistant will just plain overhear a woman tell her husband that she wishes her food weren't so salty. The server assistant will tell his server, and then the server can say, "Ah, I see by your expression that you're not enjoying your food. Let me bring you something else . . ."

Your assistant can either be your most dynamic ally or an apathetic nobody who frequently disappears when you need her most. Of the myriad things I've heard fellow servers bitch about through the years, having an inept assistant is up near the top. As fine dining restaurants usually force the servers to tip out (that is, give a percentage of their gratuity) to their assistants, servers genuinely resent having to share with people who didn't *do* their share.

However, given the right motivation and training, almost anybody can be transformed into the perfect back-server in about a week. You, as the front-server, instruct your assistant in how to greet your tables and when to pour water, clear plates, and reset. In order to get your assistant to give a damn, though, you have to appeal to his own self-interest. Let him know you'll share the wealth in a fair fashion when it's time to do the tip-out at the end of the night. And don't be tempted to screw them out of their share, either. They already know how much you made—they've been watching your credit card receipts and cash transactions all night. If you think you can pocket some extra cash by tipping your assistant less, paybacks will be a bitch when you need him to do you a favor in the future.

You see, a server assistant's job is not easy. Oftentimes, she has all kinds of people shouting orders at her, like, "Give table ten some bread," or "Clear off salads from table twenty-two right now, because their entrees are being delivered in five seconds," or "So-and-so just broke a wine glass next to a baby. Run over there right now with a broom and dustpan and clean it up!"

The server assistant has to decide which demand to meet first. If you're known to be the stingiest server, rest assured that your request will be met last every time. This means your guest will have to wait, resulting in a smaller tip for you.

Your tone of voice is also very important with your back-server. Chances are he already feels like he's the lowliest person on the restaurant totem pole. If you're demeaning or threatening to him in the way you speak, you will never get top performance out of him. Instead, strive to praise him and thank him for his hard work. Everybody likes to feel appreciated — even the busboy.

When I was a relatively new server at a prestigious restaurant in Charleston, South Carolina, I would frequently get stressed out because of the demanding nature of the job. One night in particular, I lashed out at my back-server, who didn't deserve it. I suppose he should have punched me in the nose, but instead, he just leaned in and, in his Boston accent, whispered, "You need to check your tone when speaking to me." Thank you, Evan Powell, for that polite response to my degrading demeanor.

While we're on the subject, remember this: Never have your assistant do menial work for you because you feel that you, as the front-server, are "above it."

You and the back-server are a team, and no one is getting paid the maximum unless the guest has a perfect experience.

Another huge reason not to delegate a task you could do yourself is there's a considerably higher chance that your server assistant will screw something up. You, as the front-server, already know the table number, seat number, and general mood of your table. Never take time explaining to a server assistant what needs to be done when you could have done it yourself more quickly.

If you find that you have an excellent relationship with one server assistant in particular, tell your manager that you really like working with that person. The more experiences you build together, the more flawless your service will become. In time, a well-trained server assistant can read her front-server's face like a book and silently respond without having to be verbally told what to do.

But what do you do if you're assigned a back-server who just plain sucks? This happens sometimes, and you'll be forced to give him part of your tips no matter how little he deserves it. My advice to you is to talk to management ahead of time. Tell them you have some concerns that this assistant doesn't really have his heart in it and that you will do your best to make it work anyway. Keep in mind, though, that if you're *too* bitchy, refusing to work with this person, chances are management will think you're some kind of server "diva" who will only work with the best back-servers.

If you have a bad assistant, you'll be tempted to run your mouth and tell all your coworkers what a piece of shit the back-server is. Rest assured that your smear campaign will get back to this person, and they will retaliate by mentioning any faults *you* have.

Don't do it. It's a natural impulse, but resist it. It will only make you look like a troublemaker.

Usually, the managers will already be aware of this assistant's limitations and will just be waiting to replace him as soon as they can hire someone better. Thank the manager for hearing you out and let her know you understand that not every employee is perfect. Say that you'd appreciate if this weaker back-server were rotated throughout the entire front-service staff so that you don't get saddled with this person every time.

Eventually, your managers will get so tired of hearing from everyone about this person's crappy performance that they'll take care of the situation without you having to get your fingers dirty.

In conclusion, these are the most important things to remember when dealing with your server assistant:

- Always be courteous and respectful to your assistant (no matter how stressed out you might feel).
- Share the wealth fairly when it comes time for tip-outs.
- Empower your assistant by giving her clear instructions
- If you're forced to work with a bad one, suffer through it, but let management know you'd like the rest of your server buddies to have their turn with this person before you're saddled with him again.
- Most back-servers have ambitions themselves of becoming a front-server and want to learn all they can from you. Help them.

Dealing with bartenders

In most fine dining establishments, there's a certain employee who is trained to concoct very specific drinks: the bartender.

This person's job is to receive a drink order (usually through a printed ticket the front-server has entered through a service register) and then assemble the beverages in a timely fashion. At the end of the night, a manager will look at each server's sales report and tips and allocate a certain percentage of the tips to be given to the bar staff—usually around ten percent of the overall liquor sales.

In almost every other area in a restaurant, a front-server can do everything required to make a customer happy. However, only a bartender is allowed to make alcoholic drinks, and she's usually juggling her time between dealing with live guests who tip her and the barrage of server drink tickets endlessly clicking in and printing out.

Conflict can occur when a server perceives that a bartender is taking too long to make drinks. A server might feel that his guests are waiting too long to receive their beverages, resulting in an ever-decreasing tip percentage. Then the server will start huffing and griping, causing the bartender to feel unappreciated and frustrated.

Your job as a front-server is to get your customers their drinks as quickly as possible—especially the all-important first round. See, when the guests first arrive, they're (usually) sober and very much looking forward to taking the edge off with that first sip of alcohol.

Every minute that passes before they receive that drink feels like two frustrating minutes. Even if they only have to wait for five minutes, to them, it feels like waiting ten or fifteen.

Therefore, you've got to do whatever you can to persuade the bartender to get your drinks out as fast as possible. The second round of drinks, and the third, are not as important; by then, your guests have their buzz going and are feeling good.

The wrong way to hurry up the drink order is to start complaining. It will make the bartender dislike you more than he already did. The *right* way to do it is the proactive way: the bartender needs to consider you a "friendly" based on kind actions you've done for him in the past.

So, to get the bartender to favor you above your fellow servers, try to put yourself in the bartender's shoes. Imagine what it would be like to have to do his job and have to struggle to make so many drinks at once. Ask the bartender if he needs anything. But do this quietly, face to face and under your breath, so as not to call him out for being slow. Offer to refill ice for him, bring out fresh glassware, grab more lemons from the walk-in cooler, or fetch whatever else is running low.

Even if you aren't currently waiting on any drinks to be made, be sure to check in with the bartender every fifteen minutes and ask her if she needs anything. Just like the host, she's often "chained" to her station and risks severe reprimands for leaving the bar for a mere sixty seconds just to go pee.

She may ask you to watch the bar for her just so she can relieve herself. If she does, and you're watching the bar, your most dreaded fear may come true: A person may sit down and order a drink that you're either unable or not allowed to make.

If this happens, simply grab a white cocktail napkin from the bartender's caddy and place it in front of the guest. This signals management that a bartender is waiting on the guest in a timely fashion. Next, go ahead and give the guest a glass of ice water with a little lemon slice and a straw. This tells management that this particular guest is probably cheap and not worth monitoring.

Finally, if the guest demands a certain drink before the absentee bartender has gotten back from her pee break (or unapproved smoke break), tell a manager that the bartender had to be excused, and let him make the drink for you. If the bartender hasn't returned by this point, it's on her and not on you. Bottom line: Try like hell to do every favor for the bar you can when business is slow so that when high demand eventually occurs, you'll be favored with quick drinks above other, more ungrateful servers.

And never forget this: dealing with rude and demanding customers is nerve-wracking. Unless you have Zen-like patience or experienced-server demeanor, the quickest way to calm down is to take a quick shot. It can be tempting to ask a friendly bartender for an "under the table" drink for yourself, just to settle your nerves. This actually does happen quite a bit, and your management staff already knows about it. That's why they constantly inventory the liquor levels on every bottle to see what the overall wholesale liquor cost is.

When the liquor cost starts to go up, they know someone has been stealing. Do everyone a favor and don't do it. Drinking on the job is stealing, flat out. It definitely results in a server's termination faster than anything I've ever seen.

It can also be smelled on your breath, it slows your reaction time down, and it makes you think you're slicker than you actually are—not to mention, it puts the bartender in a compromising position because he's accountable for all the booze.

It's known in the food service industry that most bartenders will occasionally sneak a drink for themselves, especially when business is extremely demanding and stressful. It's known as a "maintenance shot," and should happen only once an hour, at the most. The bartender is just trying to maintain his cool around a bunch of rude and drunk people without losing it himself. As long as he's discreet and not obvious, most managers will usually turn a blind eye.

However, just like some drug dealers, some bartenders can become their own best customers. This inevitably ends in a downward spiral that will take anybody who's nearby down with them. Sometimes, a bartender may ask you to "watch out" for her, meaning that she'd like you to keep an eye out for a lurking manager or snitch employee while she sneaks a quick drink. This can then put *you* in a compromising position of being an accessory to the crime.

My honest advice is just don't do it—but if you do, you'd better be slick. Once you get caught, rest assured that you'll be fired along with the thieving bartender. You won't be able to get any kind of reference for your next restaurant job, which is a career death sentence in an industry where reputation is everything.

Most veteran bartenders already know this and would never involve a front-server in their business anyway.

My final advice on dealing with bartenders is this:

DON'T PISS THEM OFF.

A bartender can screw over a server like nobody's business. He can make you wait forever to get your drinks. He can give you weak or watered-down drinks that will only piss off your thirsty customers. He can put the drink ticket you rang in ten minutes ago under a mound of newly entered drink orders so yours will be made last. He can even (my personal favorite) not make it *at all* and tell you that your drink ticket must have "blown away."

If you've just sent a drink order to the bar for ten different specialty cocktails, for the love of God, don't instantly go running over to the bar, saying, "Hey! Where's my drinks?!" Instead, think of this as the perfect time to go back over to your table and say something smooth like, "While our bar staff is busy perfecting your cocktails, I thought I could tell you all about tonight's specials."

This will give the bar staff the needed time to make your drinks, and will keep the guest from having to wonder where the hell you've been in the ten minutes it would take any bartender to complete your drink order. When you do finally go over to the bar to pick up your drinks, always verbally thank the bartender by name.

Make sure you can carry all your drinks securely, either by tray or hand. Nothing pisses off a bartender more than watching a server drop or spill all the cocktails he has just finished preparing.

Don't ever carry more than you're comfortable with. Get a buddy to help you drop off the drinks, or else make multiple trips.

Remember this above everything else: The bartender needs to make money just as badly as you do. Form an alliance with her to get the job done, whatever it takes.

Now look at you — you're swimming in the deep blue sea with the little helper fish (assistants) and the bigger fish (bartenders) who swarm up around the big sharks. Now, it's time to get in with the biggest fish in your pond: the managers.

The managers

More than any other factor, your relationship with the manager affects how much money you make in a restaurant. Your manager decides what shifts you work, which section in the restaurant you are assigned, how many tables you can serve at once, and which reservations go to you. His opinion of you as a server guides his decision-making process.

If you make a lot of mistakes, the manager will give you a smaller section with unimportant tables and fewer guests. If, however, guests compliment the manager on your excellent service, then you'll begin receiving better shifts, bigger sections, and wealthier guests. Therefore, it is vital to your wallet that the management staff respects you and likes you.

Even if you think you do a great job, if the manager doesn't like you, she can make each shift you work a virtual hell on earth! Personally, I don't care what it takes for you to get your manager to like you; just do it.

If you have a fat manager—particularly a female one—who is insecure about her weight, ask her if she's been losing weight, because she looks like she's slimming down. If you have a male manager who is really pushy, tell him how much you appreciate all the insight he is giving you. Say whatever it is they want to hear—and if you don't say it pretty quickly, it's very likely that your more intuitive coworkers will have already worked out the "magic code." This is not manipulation. *This is restaurant survival.*

If you can't get the manager to see you as a real person and a friend, you're fucked. Simple as that. It's incredibly easy for a manager to dislike servers, because in some cases, servers work fewer hours and earn more money through tips. So don't get on their bad side!

There are ten sure ways to piss off your manager. Never, never do these things, my darlings:

1. Call out of your shift.
2. Come in late.
3. Have a bad attitude.
4. Generate customer complaints.
5. Cause drama among the staff.
6. Ringing in orders incorrectly.
7. Lack menu/wine list knowledge.
8. Have a sloppy, unprofessional appearance.
9. Need the manager to constantly "fix" your mistakes.
10. Fail to perform necessary side work.

Now, here are ten sure ways to guarantee you stay on the manager's good side:

1. Only call out of shifts in genuine emergencies, not because you're hung over or don't feel like working.
2. Come in five minutes early every time.
3. Have a great attitude. When your coworkers say, "Hi, how are you?", always respond with, "I'm awesome!"
4. Generate customer compliments.
5. Reduce drama within the staff by staying out of conflicts.
6. Take the time to ring in your orders correctly, and always double-check them before you send them through to the kitchen.
7. Study your wine list and menu backward and forward until you feel like you could teach it to someone else.
8. Come to work neatly dressed, in a clean, pressed uniform, and be absolutely, one hundred percent, well-groomed from head to toe.
9. Learn how the manager wants things done and do them correctly the first time so that you don't need to fix your mistakes.
10. Always finish each shift by completing all of your closing duties. No one likes doing side work, but if you slack on it, it will generate animosity within the staff, and they will snitch you out to the manager the first chance they get!

So, if you can get the host stand, the server assistants, the bartenders, and the management staff to like you, you are doing pretty well. But to really start making money, you have to forge an uneasy alliance with the part of the restaurant where the shit is always hitting the fan. And this department already doesn't like you.

The back of the house

In every restaurant, there is a dual personality: the smooth, smiling face of the front of the house (i.e. servers and managers) and the red-cheeked, sweating, frustrated face of the back of the house (i.e. the chef, line cooks, and dishwashers). If you as a server are ever to succeed, you must, you *must*, convince the back of the house to respect you.

And they don't give out respect easily, either! While you're gliding through an air-conditioned and tastefully lit room, they're battling it out in a stainless-steel *sweat box with roaring flames*. If they respect you, they will usually get your ticket order completed in a timely fashion, but if you piss them off, they can make you a last priority every time.

Here, for your enlightenment, is a list of things you might do that are guaranteed to make the kitchen staff hate your ass forever:

1. Ring in orders incorrectly.
2. Have a lack of menu/food knowledge, resulting in mistakes.
3. Have unrealistic expectations of how long it takes to prepare food.
4. Drop/spill completed dishes.
5. Constantly request dishes to be modified for special orders.
6. Go on and on about how much money you did or didn't make.
7. Refuse to run your own food or other servers' food, thus allowing the dishes to get cold.

8. Beg for food or steal little bites for yourself—like pinching French fries off a plate.
9. Act superior to the kitchen staff, implying you're above/better than the back of the house. This is the number one dumb-ass suicide move that you as a server will *never* recover from.
10. Continuously screw up an order and then demand a new dish "on the fly."

And now, here's a list of things you can do to make the kitchen staff respect and like you:

1. Thank the back of the house every time they complete your order. Make sure you know all kitchen employees by their first names, and praise their hard work.
2. Limit your special requests. Don't try to redesign the menu and never, *never* ask for special requests during peak times, when the kitchen is getting overwhelmed.
3. Learn how to carry dishes correctly, whether by tray, hand, or cart.
4. Understand the menu and learn all the dishes' descriptions correctly. Don't ask for a hamburger with no pickle when your restaurant doesn't even have pickles. This tells the kitchen you're either stupid or too lazy to learn the menu.
5. Ask the kitchen if there is anything they need, like a glass of water, or to find a manager or locate a server for clarification to an order.
6. Always treat every kitchen member with respect. Even the non-English speaking immigrant dishwasher. If you just drop your dirty plates off without scraping

them, you make his job harder, and he will bad-mouth you to the other kitchen employees.
7. Learn how to time your courses correctly. This means understanding how long it takes for each dish to be made and synchronizing when you give the ticket orders to the kitchen.
8. Be professional. If you make a mistake, just admit it and don't lie! If you ring in the wrong entree, don't say something like, "Oh, the guest just changed his mind." Trust me, the kitchen has heard it all before, and they will smell the bullshit all over you.
9. When the kitchen makes a mistake, like over-cooking a steak, don't act like it's the end of the world. Instead, play it down and say, "Guys, let me know when the new steak is ready," and then just quietly leave the kitchen.
10. Try not to talk too much *or* too loudly when you're in the kitchen—especially around the head chef and line cooks, who are concentrating and multi-tasking in more ways than you can possibly imagine.

Now that you have learned how to deal with all your fellow coworkers and managers, it's time for you to fine-tune your game. One of the best and easiest ways to do this is to spruce up your appearance.

Chapter Four:
Your Appearance

I'm pretty sure you already know how you look. Chances are, you are aware of when you look your best and when you don't.

Here's the thing: you need *every edge you can get* when you're waiting tables. Your appearance is the first thing the guest notices, and it gives them all kinds of clues about what kind of person you are. You can look sloppy and dumpy and slouchy, or you can look well-groomed and clean and confident.

A lot of people in the restaurant industry feel that since a food service job is not a "real" job, they can show up looking like they just woke up. This is not the way to make the most money, people. Give yourself at least a full thirty minutes to shower, shave, do your hair, put on your makeup, whatever. Look at yourself from all sides. Use a small hand mirror and check out the back of yourself, as well. You want to walk out your front door feeling like, "Damn! I look hot today!"

It's cool to have your own look, but remember that as you deal with the public, it is in your best financial interest to look as pleasing as possible to the greatest percentage of people. For the super-expressive individuals, this means toning it down. For those who don't have much pizzazz, it means sprucing things up.

Attractive people have an advantage in most areas of life, and that goes double for life in the restaurant world. They make higher tips, get better sections, and are excused for their mistakes more often.

If you know you're a little overweight, try to do something sensible about it to lose a few extra pounds. Or maybe you can improve your smile — perhaps some whitening strips for your teeth. Do whatever it takes for you to look your best. You don't have to be the hottest person in the restaurant. Just have your personal look and own it.

A brief word or two about work apparel: Most restaurants will want you to show up in some kind of pre-approved uniform — usually, black or khaki pants and a white or black shirt of some kind. Make sure your uniform is always freshly laundered and smells clean. I have seen plenty of servers only "spot clean" their clothes between shifts. I don't know if it fools the guests, but it doesn't fool me. If you have to, throw your work clothes in the kitchen sink and do a hand load. Hang them up to dry in the shower overnight, and then give them a light ironing if needed.

While we're on the subject of the standard black-and-white server uniform, here are a couple of quick tips on how to extend the lives of those pieces of clothing. If you're required to wear a white top of some kind, odds are that you're constantly going to be getting food and wine stains all over it. The best way to fix this in the middle of a shift is with chlorine bleach. There's usually a gallon jug of it somewhere around the dish pit area. Simply pour a little bit of bleach into a cup and dilute it, half-and-half, with water. Next, dab it onto the stained area with a dishcloth. Rub it in lightly, and the stain will usually disappear immediately. Next, using only tap water, rub fresh water onto the bleached area to remove the strong chlorine smell. Otherwise, you'll smell like a public swimming pool for the rest of your shift.

As for black server pants, they tend not to show as many stains, but they are susceptible to getting bleach spots on them from daily cleaning duties. The result is a rust-colored splotch that can ruin the look of a nice pair of server pants. The easy, quick fix for this is to run and grab a black felt-tip pen and color in the area. However, this fix is only temporary and usually washes out in the laundry. A more permanent, yet cheap, solution is available at your local dollar store. Buy a jet-black hair dye kit. Just mix a little bit up and apply it to the affected area. Let it sit for twenty minutes or so, and then rinse thoroughly. Voila! A pair of server pants saved for only pennies. These two tips—using chlorine bleach and cheap hair dye—can extend the longevity of a server uniform indefinitely.

If your restaurant is open for more than just dinner, like breakfast or lunch, then God help you. Every server has had this happen at least once: For whatever reason, they went out and partied the night before their shift. Without exactly planning on it, they "crashed" somewhere and passed out in their work clothes. The next thing they remember is their phone ringing with a message from work wanting to know where the fuck they are.

In this situation, it might be tempting to just jump in the car and head to work in whatever disheveled condition you're in. However, if you show up looking like crap, your boss is likely to let you complete your scheduled shift and then fire you after all the side work is done. Remember, servers have to work in full view of the public eye. You aren't in some dark warehouse somewhere loading boxes. People can see you and will make assessments about the overall cleanliness of the restaurant based on your appearance.

Therefore, if and when it happens, don't just run into work. It's far better to be an additional ten minutes late and look presentable than to show up ten minutes faster smelling like beer and cigarettes. I have a tried-and-true emergency technique for just such occasions. I'll break it down for you in increments.

Remember, this is only for emergencies. (This wouldn't be a bad page to tear out and keep in your wallet, just in case.) I call this technique the "I-fucked-up emergency get-ready ten-minute plan":

- **Minute 1:** Turn shower on hot, full blast. Call work and tell them that you're really sorry, that your phone didn't go off and that you are on the way.

- **Minute 2:** Run to the kitchen sink and spot clean the previous night's uniform. I know I just said not to do this, but this is only for dire situations. Use diluted bleach on anything white. Get your uniform on two hangers and hang it up on the shower head as you hop into the shower.
- **Minute 3:** Scrub yourself from head to toe with soap and rinse off. Sorry, but you only get one minute in the shower. You fucked it up—deal!
- **Minute 4:** Hop out of the shower and towel off quickly. Leave the shower running hot so that most of the wrinkles in your clothes will fall out. Locate any source of caffeine and slam it down in one gulp, then run back to the bathroom.
- **Minutes 5-7:** Brush your teeth. You absolutely cannot show up to work with funky breath. If you're a guy, make sure you do a quick speed-shave. Nothing will give you away faster than a scruffy face if you're normally clean-shaven. If you're a girl, pull your hair back and slap on some lipstick. Finish up with deodorant and a healthy splash of any cologne or perfume you can get your hands on. You only get three minutes to groom yourself, so make them count and don't be overly obsessive about your hair.
- **Minute 8:** Assemble all your belongings. You may have to wear the same pair of socks, which will be gross all day but better than being fired. Find your keys, phone, and all your waiter tools.
- **Minute 9:** Get dressed and look at yourself in the mirror. Check for any obvious food stains or drips, and deal with them. Give your clothes a spray of anything that smells pleasant. I don't care if it's cologne, air freshener, or fabric softener.
- **Minute 10:** Grab all your crap and run for the front door. This is also a good time to promise yourself that you will never put yourself in this situation again—and this time you mean it.

When you arrive at work, your boss is going to be pissed. Just keep saying over and over that you're sorry and it won't ever happen again. Also, no matter how hung over or in pain you are, don't act like it. Bust your ass as hard as you can all through the shift. Your job depends on it.

Don't even tell your closest friends at work how crappy you feel. Someone will always leak it back to the manager anyway.

Hopefully, you'll never need to implement these emergency methods in the first place. That being said, if you do wake up to your boss cursing you out for being late, go ahead and take the extra ten minutes for the "I-fucked-up emergency get-ready ten-minute plan." Everyone will be glad you did. Usually, a server only has this happen because he or she was hanging out with all the crew the previous night anyway.

Let's explore that phenomenon next.

Chapter Five:
Crew Bonding

In nearly every restaurant, when you're a new employee, the staff will, at some point, ask you to hang out with them after work. Your fellow restaurant employees will want to let their hair down and relax, and this usually means grabbing some drinks at a nearby bar.

Inevitably, someone starts buying rounds of shots, and it usually ends in drunken hilarity and general debacle. It's definitely a good idea to go hang out with the staff. "Crew bonding" can have several positive effects in your server career; this free time is when you get to know fellow staff members as not just co-workers, but also as friends.

The next day at work, as the shift begins, everyone will be talking about who drank too much, who made a total fool of themselves, who went home with whom, and so forth. In my restaurant career, hanging out with the crew after work has been some of the most fun I've had. Definitely make sure you enjoy this time, but keep in mind a few words of warning, as well . . .

When restaurant people are partying, they have no brakes. None at all. Generally, they'll continue to consume drugs/alcohol until either the supply/money runs out, time runs out, or they pass out. They don't party like regular people just trying to have a good time. They drink and party like they think they will never ever get another chance to enjoy themselves.

Therefore, before the first drink is ordered, you must have an "exit" strategy — have a definite time to leave and a safe way to get home. "Oh, that's not necessary," you're thinking. "I'm only going to have one drink." Ha! I've never met a food and beverage employee who had only one drink. Once you show up at the after-hours party, it's on. All I'm saying is just be aware of it. It's going to be a blast, but you absolutely want to plan ahead — while you're still sober — how the future you, in a drunken state, is going to arrive home in one piece, safe and sound.

Never ever drink and drive, guys. Usually, none of your coworkers are going to be willing to be the designated driver, so make sure you've got the Uber or Lyft app already downloaded on your phone.

I've seen more restaurant servers go to jail for driving while intoxicated than for any other illegal offense. Usually, they also end up getting fired for all the shifts they miss while in jail. Don't be one of these people. You may not want to spend the twenty bucks to pay for a cab ride home, but it's a hell of a lot cheaper than paying the thousands of dollars in fines. Trust me on this one. If you can't afford to pay for a cab ride home, then you can't afford to be partying in the first place. Enough said.

Be very careful what you say when you're out with the crew — especially if you have a gripe with someone in the restaurant. Restaurant people love to gossip and fan the flames of drama. Even if you think you're having a private conversation with a coworker, rest assured that it will eventually get around to whomever you're talking about.

Furthermore, be aware that there's usually at least one "secret snitch" in every crew who will go and tell the manager the next day who said what.

So if one of the crew asks you, "What do you think about so-and-so manager?", respond with something like, "Oh, I don't know . . . what do you think?" and just kind of feel them out before you say more.

Finally, if you partied too hard with the crew the night before and are tempted to call out of your shift the next day, *don't do it*. Rest assured that everyone you were hanging out with feels exactly as crappy as you do. If you call out with some lame excuse, everyone will know. And trust me, someone will go over to the manager and say something like, "Oh, it's too bad Roger is sick today. It sure didn't stop him from having six Moscow mules last night . . ." Never underestimate your coworkers' ability to throw you under the bus to make themselves look better in the eyes of management.

Well, now you're cool to your restaurant coworkers; everyone likes or at least tolerates you, from the hosts and bussers to your fellow servers, from the bartenders to the managers and cooks. But one thing none of these people like is a server who is constantly fucking up and causing headaches within the restaurant.

There are several ways *not* to do this, so let's just run down exactly how you do wait on tables successfully in the first place. In the next chapter, I'm going to break it down for you as if I thought you'd never even been inside a restaurant before so that every step is addressed.

Chapter Six:
The Basics

If you're ever going to make any money in a restaurant, you've got to know the fundamentals, the ABCs of fine dining. This includes the following eleven steps:

1. How to introduce yourself to a table and get the customers to like you right from the start,
2. How to take the initial beverage order,
3. How to ring it in on the server computer,
4. How to carry a tray, balance the drinks, and serve them gracefully,
5. How to describe the evening specials,
6. How to take the dinner order, ring it in correctly, and time out the courses,
7. How to serve each course correctly and check on the guests to make sure they are happy,
8. How to clear each course,
9. How to sell desserts and coffee,
10. When and how to drop the check, and
11. How to collect payment and thank the guests.

Let's just jump right in and start up with . . .

Step 1: Know how to introduce yourself to a table and get the people to like you right from the start.

This is where you make your first impression, so don't screw it up.

What you really want to do is make sure your tone of voice sounds soothing and confident, no matter how stressed out you are. Your guests are like your babies, and you don't want to alarm them. As you walk towards your seated guests, be scanning with your eyes so that you can assess the situation. This is known in the business as "reading your table."

Are the guests at the table talking to each other? Are they busy reading their menus? Are they leafing through the wine list? Is anyone even aware that you're approaching, perhaps trying to make eye contact with you? If they're all talking and you walk up and they completely ignore your presence and keep talking, then you have three options:

- Walk away and come back in two minutes.
- Stand there silently and wait to be acknowledged.
- Go ahead with your greeting and say, "Good evening, folks, my name is Carol. Shall I start you with water?" and wait to see if anyone responds. If no one does, then walk away and come back in two minutes.

Believe it or not, sometimes guests are trying so hard to tell each other a story or get a point across that they really don't want to be interrupted, especially if the person talking is at the head of the table or is the honored guest. Always remember this: Your guests haven't come to the restaurant with a desire to interact with you, but with each other. You should always respect this wish and do your best to never interrupt your guest's conversations.

Every time you disrupt the table's flow, they will like you less and will tip you less. Strive to make them feel that you think they're the star, and not the other way around. That said, sometimes you've got to get the table started.

Even if one person won't shut up for five seconds, everyone else probably wants to get a drink order in. I like to walk up quickly with a big smile, and from about six feet away I say in a kind of loud voice, "Good evening, everyone!" I say it as if I didn't realize I was interrupting. Then I introduce myself and ask for a water/drink order. If no one responds, I just say, "Very well, then, I'll check back in a few." Then I don't go back for at least five minutes; it's guaranteed that by then, they'll be willing to interact with me.

Side note: When a server asks a guest how he is doing, the guest will oftentimes respond with the ol' "I'm fine, how are you?" When that does happen, definitely do *not* try to tell the guest how you're really feeling. Do not say, "Oh, I'm actually really tired because I've been here on a double shift all day long and I didn't even get a break." Trust me, the guest doesn't want to hear any of your complaining or whining. He only wants to know that you are okay and fine to wait on him. Just smile and say something like, "I'm great, thanks. What can I start you off with?"

Few things are more annoying to a guest than a server trying to make her feel sorry for him or involve him in his personal life. Remember, as a server, you can always walk away from the table, but the guest is stuck there in her chair. In terms of you, the server, actually telling the guest how you are, less is always more.

Step 2: Know how to take the beverage order.

Ask the table initially if they prefer bottled or tap water, and then ask if they would like to order a beverage, as well. I like to say, "What may I bring you a glass of while you're looking over the menu?" Have your pen and waiter book ready to write it all down. Don't try to remember it, as cocktail orders can sometimes be quite complicated. For instance, someone might ask for a Bombay Sapphire martini extra dry, shaken, and with three bleu cheese-stuffed olives. People are often incredibly picky and precise about the way they want their cocktails.

You want to make sure you know every liquor your place serves so that you don't take an order for something you don't have. Save yourself the embarrassment of having to come back to your table and apologize for the fact that you didn't know your shit. That will make you look like an incompetent ass right from the start. Find a list (or write one down) of all the different liquors the restaurant has so that if a guest asks for Chopin vodka, and your restaurant doesn't serve it, you can smoothly suggest an alternative vodka of equal quality and price, such as Grey Goose or Ketel One.

If the guest wants a bottle of wine, make sure you know how to open it with confidence. Buy a good corkscrew and practice on cheap bottles, or ask the bartenders if you can open some bottles for the wines that are sold by the glass.

To serve a bottle of wine correctly, start by presenting the bottle to the guest with the wine label facing the guest. While presenting it, say the wine's maker, type of wine, region where the wine was produced, and the year the wine was made. For example: Sonoma-Cutrer Chardonnay, Sonoma, California, 2009.

Then take your wine tool out, extend the small blade, and carefully place it on the bottom lip of the wine neck. With gentle upward pressure, go around the wine foil until you have made a complete circle. After the foil cap has been removed, put the cap in your pocket and not on the table. Insert the corkscrew worm (I swear to God that the little silver twisty piece of the corkscrew is known as the worm) gently into the cork and twist it halfway in until you can pry it out. Place the cork on the table so the guest can play with it.

Next, pour the guest a little sip, and when he nods, pour about a third of a glass for everyone at the table—ladies first, then the guys—and then the host last. Have a folded cloth napkin in your other hand so that after you pour each time, you can catch the little drop of wine that always drips down the side. If you don't do this, you can easily drip a little bright red spot on someone's pretty clothes. That will pretty much screw you, as the stained guest will hate you for the rest of the meal, probably demand free dry cleaning, and leave you the smallest tip ever.

After you have poured, put the bottle down, smile, and say, "Enjoy your wine." Then walk away.

Step 3: Know how to ring in the drink order correctly on the server computer.

Most restaurants will require you to "ring in" (i.e. input into a computer) your drinks before a bartender will make them. When you're a newer employee, you will be trained to do this by a veteran employee. Make sure you pay close attention. Ringing in a drink incorrectly means it will have to be remade, which will cost your restaurant money and will piss off both the busy bartender and the liquor inventorying manager. They may even make you pay for it, so get it right the first time.

Step 4: Know how to pick up your drinks securely and safely, and how to carry them on a tray.

If you've never done this before, it can look a little intimidating, so you're going to want to practice. Start off with empty plastic cups on a small server tray. Trust me on this one. Practice picking them up and arranging them on the tray with equal spacing between them. This will distribute the weight evenly and make it much easier to balance. Next, practice walking with your tray and then setting the cups down safely.

After you've successfully done this with empty plastic cups, repeat it with plastic cups filled with ice water. When you can do that, move on to real glasses. Mix it up with all different styles of glasses, like wine glasses, martini glasses, and cocktail glasses. And remember, no one wants to put his or her mouth where your fingers have been, so always handle glasses by the stem — or, if they are straight-sided glasses (like an iced tea glass), never put your hand closer than one inch from the rim.

As you serve the drinks, it is highly possible that you'll be coming up from behind your guests, who are seated with their backs to you. They may even make a sudden gesture with their arms, unaware that you're there, and knock your whole tray over. Give them some kind of verbal warning so this doesn't happen. Say something like, "Here we are, folks, I'm behind you with your cocktails." If possible, always serve beverages on the right-hand side of the guests, with your right hand, since most people are right-handed.

Never overload your tray with more than you can safely carry and deliver. It's much better to make two trips than it is to lose the whole tray. Or, better yet, get a server buddy to follow with the remaining drinks.

Step 5: Know how to describe the evening's specials.

Some restaurants will have their specials listed on the menu, and some will want the server to "verbal" them to the table. This means actually describing them orally.

If you have to talk about the nightly specials, you must memorize them. Start by writing them down, and then practice saying them over and over until the spiel rolls off your tongue smoothly. If you need to, create a specials "cheat sheet" and put it inside your waiter book. The little white slips of paper that come out of the receipt printer are the perfect size for this, as they're already designed to be slim enough to fit inside your book. Try not to rely on the written cheat sheet, though; it makes you look a little lame if you have to keep peeking in your book the whole time you're reciting the evening specials.

You will look much more professional and confident if you can recite all the evening's specials without breaking eye contact with your table. Try not to oversell the specials by saying something like, "Oh, it's the best lamb chop ever! You should get it!" Just tell them what it is and how it's prepared, and finish by saying the price.

The guest should always know how expensive something is before ordering it. Evaluating whether the special is a good deal or not is part of their decision-making process. If you don't tell them the price, then they have to ask you, which can make them feel like they look cheap or tacky. Avoid this awkwardness by simply stating the price.

After you explain the specials, tell them, "Let me know if you have any questions or whenever you're ready."

Next, wait until the table starts closing their menus or setting them down. This cue will let you know they're ready. Don't keep running over to the table and asking them if they are ready to order. This will annoy them and decrease your tip because they'll feel rushed by you.

When you sense that they're ready, you may approach the table and say, "Has everyone had time to decide?" If everyone nods, you are good to go. If someone looks uncomfortable, they may need yet more time. Walk away for two more minutes.

Step 6: Know how to take the guests' orders and enter them into the computer correctly so that each course comes out in a timely fashion.

If everyone at the table is finally ready to order, come back to the table with your waiter book and pen in hand. Otherwise, you will look really awkward fumbling in your pockets, trying to dig a pen out. At the top of your order pad, you should write down the table's assigned number and how many people are at the table. Next, you should start writing down what each guest wants from left to right, starting with the appetizer
course, then salads, and finally, the entrees.

If someone just says, "I'll have the crab cake entrée," this is the perfect time for a little of the ol' suggestive selling. All you have to say is something like, "Would you like a small salad or soup to arrive before your main course?" It works at least fifty percent of the time and gives the kitchen enough time to cook the entree.

Next, you'll have to enter all this information correctly into your restaurant's computer system. The first few times you do this, be sure to have a friendly veteran server standing by in case you get stuck and don't know how to find the correct key or button. When you've finished, double-check everything to make sure it's one hundred percent accurate. Then check it again. Once you send the information to the kitchen staff's printer, it is set in stone, and they will immediately begin to prepare your order.

Usually, restaurants will want you to "send" the entree order first, before the appetizers, to give the kitchen the required time to make the main course. However, not all restaurants operate this way, so find out how the boss wants it done ahead of time.

I cannot stress enough how important it is for you to be one hundred percent correct with ringing in your orders. Failure to do so will result in your table getting the wrong food — or someone not getting fed at all. Then the guest will become irate, and management will have to start "comping" things. In some cases, when a table has complained to the extent that food has to be given away for free to appease them, management will insist that the server pay for the meal out of his own pocket. I should know — it's happened to me. That's why I always double-check my order before sending it through to the kitchen.

With large groups, I even go ahead and print out their receipt as soon as I send it through so I can visually scan the hard copy, just to make sure everything is perfect. You may be tempted to rush through an order when you're super busy, but do not give in to the temptation. You will most certainly regret it.

Step 7: Know how to serve each course correctly and check on the guests to make sure they're happy.

To do this, it takes a little planning and preparation. Before each course arrives at the table, the server must anticipate which plateware, silverware, and condiments will be needed. You've got to do this ahead of time; no guest wants to be served a steaming bowl of soup and then have to sit there and watch it cool down while she tries to catch an employee's eye to bring her a damn spoon. And remember: If the table is going to be sharing the appetizer, they'll need you to bring them little plates to split it with.

While you're being trained in your restaurant, pay close attention to the items that are required to be brought out before each course is served. Write it down if you have to. If you have done this, when the food arrives, each guest will have everything he or she needs to enjoy it.

As you serve each plate, always try to serve the ladies first, then the guys. I know this sounds like an unnecessary pain in the ass. After all, the whole table will wait to eat until everyone has been served before anyone picks up a fork, so why bother? It's perception, people. It makes the guests feel like they're in a formal society where ladies go first. It also shows the guests that you're abiding by old-school rules—and you should be rewarded for it later. (Ka-ching!)

It is considered proper fine dining etiquette to serve food from the guest's left side, using your left hand to do it. Never put your elbow towards the guest's face. This is known in the industry as "back-handing," and is considered rude.

When every guest has been given everything he or she ordered, ask the table if they have everything they need, and then walk away.

Next is the all-important "check-back." You've got to make sure that all the guests are happy with their food and enjoying everything. The usual rule of thumb is the "two minutes" or "two bites" rule, whichever comes first. Wait until the guest has had a chance to bite into his food a couple of times before you ask him how everything is. Guests tend to get annoyed if you check back before they've even had a chance to try out their food for themselves.

As you approach the table, look at everyone's plates. Is everyone eating? If someone isn't, you likely have a problem.

Walk up and quietly ask, "Is everyone enjoying their meal?" Make sure you get a smile or a nod from everyone. If someone isn't happy, you must ascertain what's wrong and fix it as quickly as humanly possible. Although there are a million things that could be wrong with a guest's food, they generally break down into four or five major categories:

- Meat is cooked at wrong degree,
- Food arrived cold,
- Food is too salty/spicy,
- A foreign object (i.e. hair, piece of plastic) is in food, or
- Guest just plain doesn't like it.

Find out what it is that they don't like and remove the offending plate immediately. Never, *never* argue with a guest. When you do that, you're putting yourself in the position that you are right and the guest is wrong. You always want the guests to feel like you're both on the same team.

So now you have taken the plate of food away and told the guest you'll have the kitchen staff correct it as quickly as possible. When you walk into the kitchen with the plate, the back of the house staff is immediately going to be on the defensive, so don't accuse them of incompetence.

For example, if the guest ordered a filet mignon cooked medium-well and it's still red inside, do *not* say, "Hey, guys, you didn't cook this long enough." That places the blame on them, and you don't want to do that—even if it's deserved.

Remember, there are egos involved here! Instead, say, "Hey, guys, would you mind taking this up to medium-well?" Trust me, they already know they fucked up, and they don't want to hear it from you.

While you're waiting, walk back to your guest with clean silverware and replace the used fork and knife. Tell the guest her food will be coming right out and see if she needs a fresh beverage or her water refilled. Do *not* avoid this table, as it will make the guest feel like you have forgotten about her or just don't feel like dealing with her.

When you bring the item back, ask the guest if she would please go ahead and check the food. That way, you can both be sure it's prepared exactly to her satisfaction. Eventually, your guest will eat all her food and finish her course.

Step 8: Know how to clear each course.

Obviously, you will need to clear away the dirty dishes. Some restaurants will have back-servers/bussers do this for you, but even so, the server must ascertain when to begin with the cleaning.

In fine dining, the server must wait until every guest is finished before instigating the cleaning of the table. If you think everyone's done, you need to make sure before you begin, so ask them. Do *not* say, "Are you still working?" This implies that it's work to eat your restaurant's food.

Instead, say something like: "Would you like me to begin clearing your table?" or "Are you still enjoying your meal?" or "Shall I remove your plates now?" If it's a large table, and one person says, "Go ahead," then you can begin clearing. However, it's possible that some of the guests aren't aware that you've been told to begin removing plates, and they may not be finished. That's why it's important for you to ask if you're not sure. Simply say, "May I?" as you place your hand to the side of their plate.

Some guests will try to "help" you by placing their silverware to the side of their plate, signifying they are done. If they have done this, slide the silverware all the way onto the plate as you pick it up; otherwise, it's likely to fall off the plate when you pick it up and clatter onto the table, possibly splattering sauce on your guests and making you look like a complete dumbass. Try to clear from the guest's right side, using your right hand, whenever possible. This is considered correct fine-dining etiquette.

Sometimes, "helpful" guests will keep handing you plate after plate, forcing you to have to stack them up in a dangerous, unbalanced fashion. Don't do this. When you have two or three plates, and that's all you can safely carry, stop accepting any dirty plates the guests are trying to hand you. Just look at the guest, smile, and say, "I'll be right back to get the rest," and then walk away. Whenever possible, have as many assistants and fellow servers as necessary accompany you for the final clearing of the table. If you can get every item off the table in one fell swoop, your guests will be impressed.

Next, we will talk about "crumbing" the table. A "crumber" is a little metal tool that looks like a flat knife with a slightly curved edge, usually with a little handle on the side. It's used by a server to remove breadcrumbs from the tabletop.

The server holds the crumber long-side against the cloth, then drags it smoothly to the edge of the table and lets the crumbs drop into a little plate or tray. That way, the guests don't get crumbs all over their shirtsleeves as they stretch across their newly cleared table.

Why even bother crumbing? For one thing, people are used to almost every aspect of service in a restaurant, but crumbing is only done in nicer fine-dining establishments, so it stands out. It makes people feel like they are getting specialized, individual treatment—almost like an old-school shoeshine.

When you do it, be non-obtrusive about it. Don't walk up with a booming voice and say, "I will now crumb your messy table." Just quietly begin with the gentle scraping of the tablecloth. It should only take about thirty seconds. Don't try to crumb any globs of sauce, like marinara or gravy. The result will be a long, streaky smear that only makes the table look worse.

Since people aren't often used to having someone walk up and silently crumb their table, it can make them feel a little uncomfortable; they'll try to break the silence with one of two comments.

If there are a bunch of crumbs in front of a guest, he'll try to blame whoever he's seated next to by saying, "I can't believe what a big mess you made!" Have your response ready—"It's quite all right"—and smile. The other thing a guest will do is apologize because she's embarrassed that she made a mess and now you have to clean it up. She'll say, "Oh, I'm sorry I made such a mess." Your response should be, "That's okay—it's half the fun!"

One last thing about crumbing: Never scrape your crumber towards the guest's lap, only to the side of the table where no one is sitting. Be sure to always have a little bread plate to catch the crumbs so they don't litter the floor. Finally, take the bread plate back to the dish room. Don't simply wipe it off and return it to the clean pile of bread plates (as I have seen so many servers do).

Step 9: Know how to sell desserts and coffee.

When you return to the table, it is now time to sell desserts, coffee, and after-dinner drinks. Although many servers try to rush this part of the experience so they can "turn" their table quicker, this is the last chance you'll get to increase the customer's bill and overall feeling of satisfaction. So don't skip it—unless your customer already asked for the bill when the entree plates were being removed.

If your restaurant uses printed-out dessert menus, then just walk up to the table and hand them out to each guest, already opened up. After you've given them the menus, ask if anyone would like a coffee or beverage while they're considering their dessert options.

If someone does order coffee, always make sure that when you serve it, you warn your guests ahead of time by saying, "I'm coming behind you on your right side with hot coffee." And never have the coffee pre-poured in the cup, as it can cause severe burns and scalding if the coffee spills onto the guest.

Place the cup down to the right of the guest, then fill it three-quarters of the way full with a coffee urn or pitcher. Serve it with cream and a little sweetener caddy and have the coffee cup handle pointed at the four o'clock position in relation to the saucer, with the spoon at four o'clock, as well.

This is also a good time to ask for an after-dinner cocktail order. For example, say, "Would anyone like a little Bailey's Irish Cream to go with their coffee?" If you even get one "yes," you'll have increased the guest's bill by ten dollars. Be knowledgeable about what types of after-dinner liqueurs your restaurant has stocked so you can be confident with your suggestive selling.

Most good restaurants will have an expensive selection of cognacs, port wines, dessert wines, and liquors to offer. Know at least one particular type in each category.

When it's time to sell desserts, have a favorite one to recommend that you can describe in detail. Use adjectives in your description to make it all the more mouth-watering; for example, say, "The key lime pie is made with freshly squeezed lime juice, heavy cream, and cane sugar, with a crunchy butter-and-graham-cracker crust, and topped with a tart lime slice and rich whipped cream."

Most women will opt for something chocolate, and the curvy girls at the table are an almost guaranteed sell. They didn't get that sexy by saying "no" to sweets in the first place.

You can even say, "If you're too full to enjoy dessert right now, we can always box up a piece for a late-night snack."

Step 10: Know when and how to drop the check.

Once you get the dessert order and ring it in, this is a good time to carefully review the check. You'll want to check it very specifically to make sure everything is correct. As you review the guests' check on the computer, make sure you've rung in all the soft drinks, iced teas, coffees, and beverages.

The goal here is that when you drop the check off, the customer will not be able to find a single mistake. If he does, he will automatically assume it was a deliberate attempt by you to screw him over. He'll think it only fair to give you a shitty tip in retaliation. Do not give him this excuse for any reason.

And don't write any smarmy little notes on the check in an attempt to ingratiate yourself. I've seen servers write all kinds of crappy stuff on the checks, like, "It was my pleasure to serve you," or "It was nice to meet you." Your guest didn't come into your restaurant so you can pass her a note like you were in middle school. Just put the printed check inside the little check book thingy.

After your table has finished dessert and coffee, ask the guests if they would like anything else. If the answer is no, place the enclosed check book on the table and say something like, "I'll take this whenever you're ready," and walk away.

Pay close attention to exactly where and how you have placed the book so that a few minutes later, you will know if anyone has moved it — indicating that it's been opened, read, and either cash or a credit card has been placed in it.

What you don't want to do is keep coming by the table and asking if they are ready to pay out. This is highly annoying to the guest and will ruin your chance of getting a good tip. These days, almost everyone uses a card to pay, and you'll be able to see it sticking out of the check book when the guest is ready to pay.

Ask everyone how they would like their check, whether everybody's order is to be on one check, or if there are (the oh-so-dreaded) separate checks. Separate checks suck for so many reasons, but here are just a few: They take forever to process, they take longer to pay out, and — my favorite — if no one at the table has enough money to pay for the entire group, it means they're most likely cheap and will all tip you a little less due to the diffusion of responsibility. In other words, each guest assumes everyone else is taking care of you in a big way, so he or she can rationalize giving you a little less.

In some restaurants, larger groups (like eight or more) are automatically forced to be on one check, and the guests will be told this ahead of time. In addition, some restaurants will also have an "automatic gratuity" policy on larger parties so the server will not get screwed over. Usually, the amount is somewhere around eighteen to twenty percent.

If you have waited on a larger party and had the manager add a gratuity, it will show up on the printed receipt. When you set the check book down, just say, "Thank you so much. I hope you all enjoyed everything. Gratuity has been added; have a good evening."

Do not attempt to sneak in the gratuity, as I have seen *so* many servers attempt to do, in hopes of getting the "double-grat." If the guest has placed cash in the check book, don't ask him if he wants change. In effect, you're asking "Hey, is this all for me? Or do you want some back?" That puts the guest in the awkward position of having to admit that no, it's not all just for you, and she would like some of the money returned to her.

Instead, just say, "I'll be right back with your change." If she wants you to keep it all, then she'll say so at that point. If she says nothing, it means that she does indeed wish to have her change returned.

One quick note about change: Make sure you return cash in the correct bill denominations so the guest can give you a twenty percent tip. For example, let's say the guest's bill is twenty-eight dollars and he hands you a fifty-dollar bill. If you return with a twenty and two ones, he'll probably leave you just two dollars. He sure as hell isn't going to leave you a twenty on a check of twenty-eight bucks. Instead, break his money down into small bills and return with a ten, two fives, and two ones. Odds are he'll keep fifteen or so and leave you a five or six-dollar tip.

Step 11: Know how to collect payment and thank the guests.

Always thank your guests as you drop off their change and try to make eye contact and smile. Remember, this is the all-important last moment you'll have to make a positive impact on your guests, so be sure to milk it every time.

All this said, remember that you'll (hopefully) have more than one active table in your section at a time. You will need to divide your attention equally between all of your tables. To do this, the best strategy is to imitate the behavior of a shark in the wild. One never observes a shark just kind of "hanging out" in the reef. A shark is constantly prowling to the left and right, observing everything in sight.

This is how the best servers behave within their sections. You must pass through your section often and your attention must be laser-focused on all the little details that make for a memorable dining experience. Look at each guest's beverage to see if he or she needs a refill or a fresh drink. Try to notice if guests have run out of anything, like butter for their bread or sweetener for their iced tea. Has anyone pushed his plate to the side of the table, indicating that he'd like it to be removed?

Are any of your guests trying to make eye contact with you to get your attention? They will usually do this by trying to look at your face and then raising their eyebrows a little. This means your guest needs something and is trying to be polite about it without raising her hand or snapping her fingers.

As you pass by each table, try to be as nonchalant as possible. Don't just walk directly up to each table and stare everyone up and down. That's creepy as hell. If you need an excuse to go up to a table, have a water pitcher in hand as if you're going to refill their glasses. Or you can pretend to be straightening up the silverware on an adjacent table while your eyes wander over to check out what your guests might be needing.

If all is well on your active tables, feel free to go somewhere else for a few minutes. Knock out some side work or run a fellow server's food for them. Just remember—never, *never* be gone from your section for more than five minutes for any reason. If you leave your section and a moment later one of your guests decides that he needs something, he'll have had to wait until your return to request it. The longer he had to wait, the less he will tip you.

Holly, my friend and fellow server in Louisville, Kentucky, trains lots of new servers. She always advises them to stay in their sections and constantly monitor what the guests might need. "You gotta 'shark it!'," she always says.

Chapter Seven:
Food and Wine Knowledge

One of the biggest things a server can do to increase her sales is to empower herself with knowledge. This means learning everything you can about the menu where you work, as well as understanding the wines your restaurant sells. Customers will often have questions about particular items or words on the dinner menu and wine list. Being able to respond with intelligent, concise answers tells the guests that you're a professional. On the other hand, *not* knowing the answers to their questions lets them know that you're just a hack — and nobody wants to tip a hack beyond a "sympathy tip."

The best way to learn your restaurant's menu is to take one home. Read every single word. Each time you see a term you don't know, look it up on Wikipedia. If the quantity or size of a restaurant item isn't clearly printed on the menu, make a note to find out how big it is. The soup of the day, for example — is it served in a cup or a bowl? Is there an option of ordering either size? Or if a dish says it comes with a sauce, does it come on the side or directly on top of the food?

You'll also need to find out how each dish is prepared. Is it broiled, sautéed, boiled, braised, grilled, smoked, or deep-fried? And if you don't know what all of *those* words mean, stop reading this right now and look them up.

Many times, a guest will want to change how a dish is prepared for one reason or another. He'll ask if the chicken can be broiled instead of sautéed, because broiling uses no oil and has fewer calories. Sometimes your chef won't mind changing the preparation, while other chefs are super picky about how they want a dish to be presented. They will adamantly refuse to alter their creations in any way and tell you that the guest can either eat it the way it comes or order something else.

It used to be that food service employees had the upper hand when it came to food knowledge and preparation. These days, with the advent of The Food Network and other channels, many guests consider themselves "foodies." They think they know a little something about cuisine and will even quiz you on various terminologies to see if they can trip you up. Don't let them accomplish this. Be informed and educated about every item your restaurant sells, from the appetizers to the desserts.

The more you know about food, the better you'll be able to describe it in detail and the more you'll be able to sell — and thus the higher your tip averages will be.

When a new table sits down in your section, as you are greeting them, ask them if they've dined here before. If the answer is no, then ask them if they would like a little guidance with the menu. This little verbal walk-through of the menu is known as your "spiel" within the food and beverage industry. It shouldn't last more than sixty seconds, or you'll lose the guests' attention and begin to irritate them.

Start with the first page; point out some appetizers that people always rave about, highlight one or two of the more expensive salads, and describe a couple of popular entree choices that your restaurant is well-known for.

Practice this out loud at home, using a timer, until you get it just right. Stand up with a menu and look in the mirror if you have to. If it takes you longer than sixty seconds, remove something from the spiel. Repeat this over and over again until it's like saying the Pledge of Allegiance.

When you're ready, have a friend or coworker role-play as the guest while you recite your spiel. I know it feels kind of goofy to do this, but believe me, if you can't give your spiel to your BF, there's no way you're going to be able to perform it to a table full of strangers.

Learning about food is easy compared to increasing your knowledge of wine. Everyone grows up eating and thus knows something about food, but some people have never tried wine. There is so much to learn about wine that you could spend your whole life educating yourself about it and still have only scratched the surface. However, even if you don't know anything about wine at all, you can gain a working knowledge in a couple weeks.

Most veteran servers in expensive, four-star restaurants will tell you that to truly make the most money, wine knowledge is key. If a guest is going to drop a couple hundred on a bottle of wine, she will probably ask a few questions about it first. If you're just starting out as a server and don't feel comfortable taking questions about wine, then find the server or manager in the restaurant who knows the most about wine and send them over.

That said, you still need to upgrade your skill set and start learning about wine yourself. Go online and read the basics. After only about an hour of research, you can learn the different varieties of white and red wines.

The other part of the equation is understanding wine and food pairings. The general idea is that some types or varietals of wines make certain foods taste better when consumed together. Most experts like to say that a nice red wine, like cabernet sauvignon, goes well with steak, or that chardonnay goes great with grilled chicken. The basic rule is that red wine goes with red meats and red sauces, and white wine goes with white meats and white sauces. These are only guidelines, however. No "wine police" will show up and arrest someone for drinking a white pinot grigio with his rack of lamb.

Remember, an iced tea sells for about two bucks, and a cheap bottle of wine goes for at least twenty-five. Therefore, there is *never* a bad reason to sell a bottle of wine to your table. If you're waiting on a table of two people and they each want only a glass of wine, remind them that it's often a better deal to buy a bottle and share it. Having a bottle of wine on the table also increases the guests' overall feeling of satisfaction and creates a sense of occasion to the meal.

To further increase your understanding of wine, at some point you are going to have to start tasting some. Ask your manager if your restaurant ever has wine tastings to educate the staff. Most do. If not, see if your manager will pour you a tiny drop in a glass so that you will be better able to describe it to your tables.

If the manager says yes, make sure to have a little pad of paper and pen handy so you can write down your particular impressions of the wine. This will show the manager that you're sincere about becoming a better server—and not just trying to score a free swig.

Even if you upgrade your wine knowledge and manage to convince your table to order a bottle of wine, problems can sometimes occur. The first is that you go to get the bottle only to find your restaurant has sold out of it. This is frustrating for you, but even more so for the guest who spent at least five minutes trying to find the perfect bottle for his needs. If this happens, don't panic. Most guests pick out a certain bottle because of the varietal or type of wine it is, where and when it was made, and how much it costs. If you're out of the particular wine the guest ordered, grab the wine list. Look and see how much that the chosen bottle costs and try to find another one that's the closest to the original in price, region, vintage, and when it was made. That way, when you go back to the table, you can say something like, "It seems that we've sold the last bottle of the wine you picked out, but I did notice that we have this bottle in stock, which is the closest in price and structure to the first bottle. Would you like to give it a try?" They usually go for it.

The other potential problem is that you open the bottle of wine for the guest, they try a little sip, and they don't like it. This will happen to you at some point, so you need to know ahead of time what your restaurant's policy is on it.

Most restaurants will tell you to take the bottle away and offer to get the guest a different bottle. Then the restaurant will send the bottle back to the wine distributor, saying that it was "corked" or contaminated with air, and receive full reimbursement for it.

That isn't always the case, however. I've worked for some real assholes who have tried to tell me that if I opened a bottle of wine for a customer, either I or the guest was going to have to pay for it. If you're forced to work in this kind of place, when a guest dislikes a bottle of wine, go and get the manager. Let the manager convince the guest to try the wine again or to give the wine a little time to "breathe" so that its true flavor will develop. If the guest still doesn't like the wine and the manager is telling you that it's all your fault, do yourself a favor and go work somewhere else.

Knowledge is power. The more you know about all the food and wines your restaurant sells, the more impressive and credible you'll appear to your tables. Whenever there's some downtime at your restaurant, question the senior staff about the menus. Ask them what kind of wine they would recommend with this or that food. Ask them where the fish comes from. Ask them what they think the best dishes are on the whole menu. Find out if there are certain dishes that tend to generate complaints, like if most people find a dish too salty or spicy. That way, you'll understand what the real crowd-pleasing items are and can steer your guests towards them.

One last thing: Don't bullshit your tables if you don't know an answer to a question. Yes, it's embarrassing to have to admit you don't know something that's part of your job. However, if you think you can make up something slick on the spot that sounds good, be warned. Once the guest has learned that you lied, the whole meal is going to go to shit. They will want to speak to your manager, and so on. When a guest asks you a question that you just don't know the answer to, the best thing to say is, "You know what? I'm not one hundred percent sure about that, but I can find out for you, and I will be right back."

Look, it's called the food and beverage industry, so learn all you can about the food and beverages your restaurant sells. You owe it to yourself to be as educated and empowered as you can be. It will do more than just improve the quality of your tips. It can even improve the quality of your life.

Chapter Eight:
The Six Magic Words

You know how in a certain board game there's a "get out of jail free" card that you can save for a rainy day? Well, I have something for you that's something like one of those cards. In a restaurant, sometimes a manager or owner can behave irrationally. Managers are human — vulnerable to stress, overworked, and under-slept. Eventually, most of them become burnt out.

At some point, you, as a server, will come under fire for something that has nothing to do with you. You will be in the wrong place at the wrong time, and the manager will start screaming at you for something absurd:

"Every time you work the patio, it rains!"
"I can't go to my own sister's wedding this weekend because I have to stay here to babysit you bitches!"
"I've told you a thousand times not to let the owner see you come through the front door!" (Even though the back door was locked and no one would buzz you in.)

It would be completely natural for you to want to defend yourself in a situation like this. You'd certainly have every right to. Still, try to resist. Even though you're right, if you start defending yourself, your manager won't hear the logic of your case. All he'll hear is that you're arguing with him instead of complying. Trust me, he'll just start yelling, and then it will get worse.

Here's the "get out of jail free" card: There are six magic words you can say that will make it all go away. Six little words that will turn the wrathful eye of Sauron from you — and onto someone else. If you forget everything else I've tried to teach you in this book, remember these words. When the manager comes up to you one day and starts yelling at about something that you have no idea about, like, "I told you to make sure the PH balance in the lobster tank was below six point five," say these words very slowly:

"You're right."
"I'm sorry."
"Thank you."

I know it may sound trite but believe me — these words are battle-tested and they work. Why? I'll break it down for you.

Step 1: Saying **"you're right"** tells the manager right away that you are in agreement with her. This starts turning the hostility down immediately, as your manager feels you are complying with whatever insanity she's going on about.

Step 2: Take a pause, then say, **"I'm sorry."** Whether or not you even understand what the manager is upset about, this tells him you're aware of the infractions and have now been corrected. This will usually shut the manager right the hell up.

Step 3: Take one more pause and say, **"Thank you."** This makes the manager feel that you're grateful she has taken time out of her busy day to verbally abuse you. It further tells her that you two are back on the same team again, and that while you may have been in error before, you have been successfully corrected and are appreciative of it.

Several times over the course of my waiting career, I've had a manager come up to me and start yelling. I learned that if I actually said these words sincerely (even if I didn't *feel* them) and looked him in the eyes, I could actually start walking away as I said them.

Remember, every time your manager looks at you, he's seeing you as part of the overall restaurant-machine. He is going to see you as either a shiny piston, pumping away to make the restaurant money, or as a broken part that either needs to be repaired or replaced. Trust me, you don't want to be repaired. It hurts. So when your crazy manager thinks he has to repair you, you can make it all stop with those six little words. You're right . . . I'm sorry . . . thank you.

Okay, so that's your "get out of jail free" card with management. Now I'll give you a couple more you can use on the customer when the shit really hits the fan.

Let's say you've been told already that the restaurant is out of something—say the halibut special. Maybe you've come into work with a fuzzy hangover, or you were a little stoned during the server meeting, so a customer orders the halibut and you forget the restaurant is out. You ring it in and the kitchen sees the ticket, and they start yelling for the manager.

The manager comes in and is like, "What the fuck?!" Then he sees you and says, "I told you we were out of the halibut!"

Then you have to go back to the table and explain to the guest that you were a complete dumbass . . . or do you? Actually, you do not.

Instead of saying, "Oh, I'm sorry, I completely forgot that we ran out of halibut. Would you mind looking over the menu and deciding on something else," you say, "Pardon my interruption, sir, but our chef is very picky. He says he doesn't like the way the halibut is smelling is refusing to serve it. Would you mind selecting something else?" This will take all the blame off of you, and make the customer feel like you're watching out for him. It works every time.

Now let's say that the main course is being served to your table and the French fries a guest ordered did not arrive. You rush over to the computer to check their order and discover that while you thought you rang it in, in fact, you didn't. You enter it in the computer as fast as you can with a little message attached, like "please rush."

You could go back to the table and say, "Oh, I'm sorry, but I forgot to ring in your fries. It's going to take at least five minutes. I'm sorry for ruining your meal." That will make your table hate you. Or you could say something like, "Hi folks, I hope you're all enjoying your meal. I noticed when they were bringing out your order that the French fries looked a little burnt, so I sent them back. They're making a fresh batch right now, and I guarantee when they hit the table they'll be piping hot! They'll be right out; in the meantime, can I get anybody anything?"

See how this works? You just push the blame off of you, and make it sound like you're doing your best to protect your customer's interest.

How about this one: Your customer ordered a Budweiser draft beer, you rang it in, but then forgot to take it to him. After about five minutes, the bartender says to you, "Hey — you want this beer or not?" "Oh, shit!" you think. The customer is going to be pissed now, so you could say, "Gee, I'm really sorry, I know you've been waiting five minutes for this beer, but I completely spaced." Or you could say, "Here's your beer, sir. Thank you for your patience — we had to change the keg." Get it?

Say the customer asked for her salad to have the dressing on the side, and you forgot to include that information when you sent the order to the kitchen. The salad comes out all gooey with dressing, and the customer says, "I told you I wanted my salad to have dressing on the side!" You could say, "Oops! My bad . . . uh, let me go get you another one," and look like a complete dumbass. Or you could say, while clucking your teeth and rolling your eyes, "I'm sorry (in a sympathetic tone). I told them to put your dressing on the side. I'll be right back with another one. In the meantime, if anyone else at your table would like to enjoy that salad, feel free. It's on the house."

Just be careful — if you have to bend the truth a little, make sure it doesn't bite you in the ass. Never say something to a guest that they can repeat back to a manager in a complaint that will get you busted. Unfortunately, many guests know they can get items "comped" or given to them for free if they keep bitching long enough.

Let's say your guests have been waiting too long for their main course. Maybe the kitchen is slammed, or perhaps one of the cooks is hung over (again), or God only knows why, but it has been more than thirty minutes since your table ordered their dinners and the food still isn't there. You could say, "I'm really sorry it's taking so long, guys. I'm doing my best to make sure your food is coming out next" (which will only irritate your table). Or you could say, "I just checked on your order and the chef is putting the finishing touches on it as we speak. In the meantime, I have brought you each a little palate-cleansing sorbet. See if you can guess the flavor!" It doesn't really matter what flavor it is—every restaurant has some kind of frozen crap they use to garnish desserts.

Okay, so now you're starting to get the hang of it, right? The customer orders a bottle of merlot that has been eighty-sixed (meaning put on the "out of stock" list). After searching for this particular bottle for five minutes, you could come back to the table empty-handed and say, "I'm really sorry, I searched like crazy trying to find the bottle of wine you wanted, but we must have run out of it. Now I need to interrupt your meal by handing you this big wine list again and make you read all the choices again and pick another one out. Oh golly, I sure hope we have whichever one you pick out this time—I guess we'll know in another five minutes."

Or . . . drum roll, please . . . you could say, "I discovered that we sold the last bottle of Cape Diamond merlot, but we do have this lovely bottle of Californian Crooked Row merlot, which is the same vintage and I think a great value at nine dollars less than the Cape Diamond."

They go for it every single time. So you see, stop thinking about these issues as problems, obstacles, and difficulties. There are only *challenges* and *opportunities*. All this said, there are some times when a server just gets overwhelmed with all the guests' demands. Every one of us is a ticking time bomb. When a server loses control of his emotions, he's vulnerable to a "screw it!" state of mind.

This is a very dangerous condition that I like to call "losing it."

Chapter Nine:
Losing It

They say that stress is an equation based on demand versus control. This means your stress level is caused by how much demand or pressure is placed upon you, and then how much control you feel you have over your situation to meet that demand. There are very few professions than waiting on tables that have more demand with less control.

The server cannot control the strength of the cocktails, the quality of the food, the temperature in the restaurant, or the rotation of the earth, for that matter. This, however, has never stopped a guest from demanding it from her server. Over-repeated exposure to demanding and demeaning guests can cause even the most patient of servers to "crack" at some point. This is also known as "losing it." It's happened to me once or twice, and I've seen it happen to many others in my twenty-five-year career of serving. The following are just a few examples of what I'm talking about. All names have been changed to protect the guilty.

Salmon-Ella

My friend and fellow server Bryce, in Phoenix, Arizona, was waiting on a woman who asked, "Does the salmon taste . . . *fishy*?" Now, everyone knows salmon is one of the fishiest tasting options of all seafood, and I guess my poor ol' buddy Bryce had had enough of dumb customer queries for one life. So he responded with, "No, it tastes like a *fucking pizza*." (Amazingly, he still kept his job.)

The Bad Potato Story

This server (and it was probably not me) had a group of fifteen people coming into his section later that night, so his manager gave him a small table of three people about an hour beforehand, just to give the server something to do until the large group arrived. After all, what could go wrong with a simple little three-top? They were a middle-aged couple taking the woman's mother out for a pleasant evening — except that the mother-in-law was anything but pleasant, and impossible to please. Maybe she was just a lonely old lady craving attention, or maybe she was just a bitter old battle-ax looking to make the rest of the world as miserable as she felt. No one will ever know.

She came into the restaurant with a big ol' chip on her shoulder. From the moment she came in, she complained about everything: The chair cushions were too cushiony and hurt her back. The lights were too dim for her to read the menu. The ice cubes made loud clinky noises in her glass. The music was not her style, the bread was too crusty, the butter was too buttery. The server couldn't get more than five feet away from the table before she started yelling "WAITER!" to add her latest disappointment to the list.

Luckily, this server had no other tables at the time and could afford to lavish the old lady with his undivided attention. She sent back her soup (too salty), then her salad (lettuce was bruised). When she finally received her prime rib dinner, the hopeful server asked how everything was, and she replied, "Fine, it's fine. Leave us alone." As if the server had been interrupting their meal for his own personal enjoyment.

Thankful, the server was able to walk away from the table of three at last, relieved that the old lady was finally satisfied, just as the group of fifteen businesspeople sat down in his section. As he approached the large table, he began to recite his usual table greeting: "Good evening, everyone! Welcome, my name is—" when he was interrupted by a scream of "WAITER!" so loud and screechy that he visibly flinched. The old lady was at it again—apparently angry that the server was cheating on her by having another table. He turned his head to face her and said quietly, "Yes, ma'am, I'll be right with you."

He then turned back to his large table and began again. "Anyway, folks, as I was saying, I want to welcome you all, my name is—" "WAITER! WAITER!" the old hen screamed again. The server, now even more embarrassed, looked at her and pointedly said, "I. Will. Be. Right. With. You." He attempted to greet his large table one last time.

As he faced the group and took a deep breath, the old woman began pounding her fist (fork in hand) as loudly as she could on the table, making all the dishes jump, as she screamed, "WAITER! NOW! NOW! NOW!"

The server looked at his fifteen-top and said, "Folks, I'm terribly sorry. I will be right back."

As he walked the mere five feet to the old woman's table, she stared at him with glowing eyes and a victorious smile. He went up to the table, put his palms flat against the tablecloth, and leaned down directly into the woman's face. He said through clenched teeth, "Yes, ma'am! What seems to be the . . . *emergency*?!"

Without missing a beat, she responded, "I think I have a bad potato."

At this point, something very fragile and precious cracked within the waiter's soul. A terrible pain ripped through his very psyche. That is exactly when a crazed gleam appeared in the waiter's eyes, and he responded, "You know what? I think you're right. I think you *do* have a bad potato!"

The old woman then jabbed her dinner fork into the baked potato and shook it in her server's face. "What are you going to do about it?" she demanded.

Then the server, bare-handed, grabbed the potato off her fork and placed it in the palm of his left hand. He raised his right arm up, and with a mighty swing, he *spanked* the potato, over and over again. "*Bad* potato! *Bad* potato!" he snarled. "Bad, bad, BAD potato!" Chunks of white, steaming potato flew from between his hands like exploding shrapnel. Then he placed the flattened potato skin back on her plate, leaned in very closely to the old woman, and growled, "Ma'am, I don't think this potato will give you any more trouble, but if it does, you just *let me know*."

The old lady just gaped at him in horror and silence as the server walked back to his waiting fifteen-top—who were applauding. The husband, wife, and mother-in-law finished their meal shortly after, and of course, the old lady paid and left no tip. As they all exited the restaurant, the husband walked up to the server and whispered, "Best meal I've had in years," and palmed him a hundred-dollar bill. True story.

So in that case, "losing it" actually worked out for the server, but it sure doesn't usually. Losing it happens when a server gets over-exposed to customers' never-ending demands.

Restaurant managers will always strive to over-schedule their star servers. They always want you to work too many shifts, back to back, without enough time off in between, and you eventually get burned out. You can even get to the point where, as soon as customers walk through the front door, you instantly resent them.

You're mad at them because you know they're going to want stuff from you. This is the point where you have lost the battle. Everyone is only human, and it's not always easy feeling like someone else's servant. "Do this. Don't do that. Maybe I'll leave you a nice tip, maybe not." It can feel toxic sometimes.

Being a server means taking care of the needs of others and not your own. No, it isn't an altruistic profession, but one of self-interest, where you hope to be rewarded for completely satisfying the needs of others.

I think of my exposure to customers sort of like radiation. Let's say I was an X-ray technician, for example. To do my job and make money, I have to put myself in a situation where I am vulnerable to X-rays. I have to put on my lead vest to protect myself from the damage of repeated exposure. Sure, I could just stay home and not worry, but then again, I don't make any money staying at home, and I need money to live.

In food service, your lead vest is time off. Downtime is when you don't have to please anybody. Don't let your restaurant work you so much that you get burned out. Unfortunately, in most restaurants, the harder you work, the more you will get worked. Be realistic and talk with your manager about how many shifts a week you can pull.

Let her know that you always want to come into work with a great attitude, and that to do that, you need x amount of time off. I strongly recommend you have at least two full days off per week from your restaurant job—preferably back to back. Don't let yourself become the bitter server who hates his job and blames the world for the fact that he has to wait on others. If you do, it's a guarantee that you won't keep your job long, anyway.

Chapter Ten:
Safety First

Let's talk a little about safety, because you can't make any tips if you keep injuring yourself over and over. A restaurant can actually be a very dangerous place to work. In the kitchen and dish pit areas, the floors are constantly wet and have invisible spatters of grease on them. Also, you're carrying hot plates, sharp silverware, and fragile glasses.

On top of all that, several of your co-workers are running around like chickens with their heads cut off — and they're fully loaded with the same ammo as you. You can get burned by hot plates, scalded by steam, cut by a kitchen employee walking with a knife blade exposed. Doesn't all this sound like fun?

And these are just the potential *accidental* injuries. There are just as many injuries you can get by repetitive motion — like carpal tunnel syndrome from carrying heavy trays with your palm flat. You can get bruised feet, varicose veins, and blown-out knees. There are, however, ways to minimize your risks.

We'll start with your feet and work our way up. Shoes are your most important piece of equipment. Most veteran servers spend between one hundred and two hundred dollars for professional restaurant clogs. If this is out of your budget range, just be sure that whatever shoes you pick, you keep these three features in mind:

- Deep tread for traction on wet tile floors,

- Good arch support (you are going to need it), and
- Deep padding to cushion your feet.

A server is like a racehorse in that you're no good if you can't run. And remember—they put down lame horses. In addition, if servers at your restaurant are required to wear black socks, I suggest putting on a pair of thick, white athletic socks underneath for added cushion and sweat-wicking.

I actually like a pair of black work shoes that Walmart used to sell (and might still online). It was a Faded Glory shoe, and the model name was Marvin. They cost about twenty bucks and usually last me around six months before their tread is worn away.

Ladies, especially—do not be tempted to wear cute little heels to make you look and feel sexy. There is nothing sexy about your agonized face as you walk around feeling like someone is driving nails into your soles. At the very least, make sure you put a cushiony insole inside your shoe for added padding. Whatever shoe you decide on, make sure you can stop on a dime in them if you have to. Your very life may depend on it.

I have seen so many spectacular falls taken by fellow servers in my time—truly epic, feet-up-in-the-air, spine-first impacts on wet kitchen floors. A truly bad fall can break bones and spinal columns. And you *are* going to fall at some point. Everyone does.

If you begin to feel yourself falling, throw anything you're carrying far away from you. It's going to be bad enough when you hit the floor; you don't want to land on broken dishes, glasses, and pointy silverware when you do.

The kitchen can always make another dish. And it's a hell of a lot cheaper to do that then it is to pay a five-thousand-dollar hospital bill from when a doctor has to pull a salad fork out of your ass.

That's one way you can fall. Then there's my favorite: the collision. Collisions occur when two restaurant employees are both in a huge hurry, and at least one of them is distracted and turns his head. It only takes a split-second, like somebody calling your name. You glance to the side while walking fast, and the other employee changes speed or direction, and *wham*! Plates go flying straight up into the air in a glorious racket.

Another good one (and my personal favorite collision) is when two servers are both moving very fast in a straight line and the one in front suddenly remembers something urgent he forgot to do and slams on the brakes. The following server, unaware of the impending doom, slams straight into the back of the now-still leading server. Ouch!

The third type of collion occurs around a blind spot, like on the edge of a doorway at the entrance of the dish pit. Servers are always in a great rush to both drop off their dirty dishes and to get out of the dish pit and back onto the floor, where they can make money. While one server is fully loaded with plates on the way in, the other server is glancing at his waiter book to verify an order—and *crash*! Both parties collide.

To avoid all this collateral damage, remember these three things:

- When you're walking fast through the restaurant, always look straight ahead.

- If you do suddenly realize that you need to stop walking, pull over. This means move a couple of feet to the right or left before you stop so a person following you won't be forced to slam into you.
- When you cross through doorways or around corners, always call out a warning, like, "Coming through" or "Corner!" If you have hot pans, yell out, "Hot! Coming through—hot!"

Sometimes, even with the best of intentions and training, collisions will occur. Yes, it is probably one party's fault more than the other, but this no time to play the blame game. If someone goes down onto the floor, treat it just like an actual accident scene, because it is. Don't try to move the person at all, even if you both think everything is okay. Go and get the manager as fast as you can.

Since crashes are inevitable, you don't want to accidentally cut someone when it happens. To prevent this, whenever you're carrying something sharp, like a knife or fork, always point the blade down and backward. That way, even if you do bump into somebody, the blade will always be turned the other way.

That's my advice on avoiding accidental injuries in a restaurant. Repetitive motion injuries require a slightly different strategy. Good shoes and supportive socks are your best defense against sore feet, varicose veins, and blown-out knees.

As far as carpal tunnel is concerned, you can get it from always carrying a heavy tray with the same hand. See if you can switch it up, and every time you have to pick up a heavy tray, alternate which hand you use. This will cut the wear and tear on your hands and wrists in half. Even if you aren't very confident using your less dominant hand, practice with an empty tray until you can. Believe me, you'll be glad you did.

There are more ways to be injured in a restaurant than there is space to write them all down, but remember this: If you do get hurt in some kind of accident, always tell your manager as soon as possible. They will have you fill out something called an "incident report," which is a legal record of how it all happened. Then, if you require any kind of medical care because of the accident, a form of insurance called workers compensation will cover it, and you won't have to pay a cent.

There are also tiny beings in a restaurant that are out to get you: microorganisms that spread through the air and by direct contact. Germs. During each shift you work, you'll be constantly handling dirty plates, glasses, and silverware that have been contaminated by human beings carrying an assortment of bacteria and viruses. You touch the dirty silverware and then scratch your nose—voila. The rhinovirus has been successfully transmitted. Your best defense is to wash your hands with soap and water throughout your shift. Try to do this at least once an hour.

Beware of trash cans in the bathrooms. If it's part of your side work to empty out the trash cans, be very careful. You *never* want to reach into the trash bag. There could be a used hypodermic needle lurking under an innocent brown paper towel. There could be used feminine hygiene products. Instead, just carefully pick up the trash can and tip it over one of the large, gray kitchen trash cans. Make sure you hold the can on the outside and not the rim so that none of the contents can touch or cut you.

Speaking of getting cut, you will occasionally be required to pick up broken dishes and glass fragments. It will be tempting to try to do this by hand, but don't. Take the time to find a broom and dustpan and sweep up the broken bits. If a chunk is too heavy to be moved by the broom, grab a paper towel to protect your hand as you pick it up. This may seem inconvenient but trust me — none of your guests will be happy if you're dripping blood on them and their food.

Also, beware of burns, people. A lot of restaurants send out dishes that have been baking or broiling until they are red-hot. Always have a napkin folded in your pocket or tucked into your belt; you can use it like an oven mitt to insulate your hand as you handle these hot dishes. And for the love of God, be sure to warn your guests whenever you are setting down a hot plate.

My final words of wisdom on safety regards the health of others. If you know you're genuinely sick, don't come into work. Most restaurants will tell you that you "have to" come in and work unless you get a fellow employee to cover your shift. This is a complete load of crap. If you do come in when you're not well, all that will happen is you'll infect your coworkers and guests.

Your coworkers can't afford to miss work because of illness any more than you can. Your paying guests have the right to dine in a safe environment, as well. We all have a duty to *not* knowingly expose each other to the threat of infection.

Tell your manager as soon as you start feeling funky so that if you do come down with something, he has been forewarned and won't just think you're trying to cover up for a hangover.

My own personal favorite call-out line you can use without having a doctor's excuse is this: You're experiencing "projectile diarrhea." Works every time. My buddy Lenny even once told the boss he couldn't come in because, as he put it, "I'm pissing out of my ass." Do what you gotta do, people.

Chapter Eleven:
The Joy of Side Work

When customers enter a restaurant, they see the wait staff serving drinks and taking orders and think this is all those employees have to do. They have no idea the staff arrived three hours earlier and will be there three hours later doing something known as side work.

Side work is all the tasks the server must perform before, during, and after meal service that are necessary for the proper functioning of the restaurant. These are things the server must do in addition to waiting on guests.

The activities before service include mopping the floors, vacuuming the carpets, wiping out chairs, sanitizing the bathrooms, rolling silverware inside napkins, lighting candles, setting all the tables, cutting butter, cleaning windows, wiping down menus, folding napkins, and polishing all the glassware and silverware.

During service hours, side work may include restocking ice, distributing freshly washed silverware, dishes, and glasses, answering the phone, carrying other servers' tables' food, bussing dirty tables, re-setting tables, heating up bread, greeting guests at the host stand, and whatever else the manager tells you to do.

After service hours are over comes the dreaded closing side work, which is usually like opening side work in reverse.

You have to clear everything off the tables and get them ready for whatever meal comes next, clean the floors, empty all the trash from the restrooms, put away all the dishes, re-polish all the glassware and silverware, clean up the coffee station, wipe down all the counters, clean out the bread warming area, and so on.

Here's the thing about side work: Every server has to do it, and no one likes it. Any server would prefer it if she could come right in when the restaurant opened, do nothing but wait on guests, and leave as soon as she got her tips. Having to come in early and stay after is especially frustrating because the server knows she isn't even getting paid minimum wage to do it. In most states in the USA, servers only get paid two or three dollars an hour by their employer. Of course the server feels exploited by having to perform all this manual labor for less than a fair wage.

But that's just the way it is. So take a deep breath and just accept it. None of your fellow servers wants to do side work, either. Before, during, and after service, servers are watching each other with great suspicion to see if everyone else is doing his or her share of the grunt work.

If one server even suspects that another server might not be doing enough allocated side work, the shit hits the fan. The offended server will start by bitching to other servers, saying things like, "Beverly never brews more coffee after she serves it! She just finishes it off and then leaves the empty pot right on the warmer to burn up!" or "Roger didn't fold his share of napkins. He just carried some around that Sue had already folded," or "James didn't polish those glasses. He just restocked them behind the bar with water spots all over them."

All this bitching will then get back to the accused server, who will either blatantly deny it or start counter-attacking the accusing server, like, "Hoo, boy, that's funny. I polish more glassware around here than anybody. I'm just faster than everyone else. Besides, John always hightails it outta here as fast as he can without even asking if everything has been done!"

In some restaurants, closing side work must be assigned specifically and then "checked off" on a side work list by a manager or closing server before you're allowed to leave.

Most veteran servers will begin doing the closing side work long before the end of the night. They do this by multi-tasking. For example, every time they go into the dish pit, they bring out a rack of glasses to be polished—one less thing to do at the end of the shift. Or they start wiping everything down as the night progresses. That's one way to cut down on how long it takes to get the hell out of Dodge, but be warned.

I've seen some servers who are so overly concerned about getting out as quickly as possible that they focus more on the required closing duties than they do on their paying customers. This is the tail wagging the dog, folks. Remember, you don't make money doing side work, you make money from guests who are so happy with your service that they leave you really nice tips.

It only takes the guest an instant to realize that he needs something, like a soup spoon or another drink. If you, the server, are in the back polishing glasses for fifteen minutes and the guest can't spot you, he's going to be pissed—and a pissed-off guest equals no money for you, no matter how much free side work you've done.

My general rule of thumb is that if you know you're going to be away from your section for more than three minutes, have a fellow server buddy of yours keep an eye on your tables for you. That way, if your guest starts rubbernecking around, your buddy can go up to him and give him whatever he needs.

Side work sucks. That's the truth. But it can also be some pleasant, non-stressful downtime in the food and beverage industry. You can have a nice, quiet chat with your coworkers as you all finish up. Everyone will be talking about how their shift went, how much money they did or didn't make, and which bar everyone is going to meet up at after work. Just don't forget to get all of your required duties done first, or you'll have to hear about it from your manager the next day.

Also, if there's one specific side work task that every other server avoids, go ahead and volunteer for it. Chances are that you can do it slowly and only have done half as much side work as everybody else. Most servers race through closing side work. A lot of them are addicted to some chemical substance they're jonesing for. Whether it's nicotine, alcohol, or whatever, they can become irate when they need their fix. You'd be surprised how many of them will even pay you an extra five or ten bucks to re-set their last table just so they can leave an extra fifteen minutes earlier or go smoke a quick cigarette. Easier money was never made.

Yep, side work sucks for sure, but without it, there would be no tip work at all, so just be smart about it. Nobody likes shaving his or her legs, either, but that's the necessary side work to look sexy (at least for some guys/girls).

Chapter Twelve:
Don't Make Honey Where You Make Your Money

Ahh, love. The sweet longings of one heart for another. Normally, on earth, this is a natural and positive response based upon mutual attraction. However, in a restaurant, it's a recipe for disaster *every fucking time*. And why is this? you may ask. Why must it be this way?

Let me break it down for you, my guys. In a restaurant, most of the staff is fairly young, in their 20s or 30s. Everyone's in his or her physical prime of life—including their libidos. Put them all in an enclosed space and do the math.

Then there's the emotional bonding that naturally occurs between restaurant folk because of common shared experience. Every day, everyone on the staff gets bombarded with needy guests and harassed by management. This creates a sort of "Hey, we're all stuck in this prison together" type of feeling. It makes the staff feel close to each other, because they know they're all going through the same thing.

Next, factor in the strange reality that all restaurant staff is on a different time schedule than the rest of the world. They get up later and stay up longer. Frequently on the weekends, when their peers are out partying, they're still toiling away inside the restaurant. So, in a sense, they're cut off from the rest of society. While others are dining out, they are refilling iced tea and serving soup. So that cuts down on the pool of people servers can hook up with.

Therefore, you've got all these young, sexy people working together and emotionally bonding every day, with limited access to the outside world, and only on each other's clocks. Attraction is natural, and servers will be drawn to each other. Still, do your best to resist, oh my children, or you will surely regret it.

Here's why. Let's say you start off in a new job at a restaurant as a server. If you're even halfway good-looking, your fellow servers will send someone over to find out what your score is—meaning are you straight or gay, single or married or involved. In other words, are you "up for grabs?"

They won't just come right out and ask it directly, though. They'll ask you coy questions like "did you move out here alone?" or "I can't believe a pretty girl like you doesn't have a boyfriend," or some other lame-ass line to fish it out. Then, if one of the staff likes you or has a crush on you, they'll get one of their coworkers to find out if you like them back. The coworker will ask you, "I think Roger's kinda cute, don't you?" or "Michelle has such a pretty smile, don't you think?" Then he'll wait and see if he can get some kind of reaction out of you, like, "Oh, yeah, I guess," or "Not really," that he can then report back to your secret admirer.

Let's say two servers start sleeping together. This will still cause problems at work right away for a couple reasons. First, a person goes to his job to work, not to be all lovey-dovey with his boo. Second, one of the two is likely to be the jealous type, and the other is even more likely to be the cheating type.

Even if the relationship starts off well, it can still cause problems within the staff. The two servers will start asking the manager to schedule their days off together so they can see each other when they're off.

Or they'll start pestering fellow servers to switch shifts with them so they can have time together. Then, when they're both at work, they will constantly stop working so they can "check in" with each other. You know, just to make sure the other is having an okay night.

Restaurant work can get very hectic very fast. Nerves get frayed, and the next thing you know, Angie is mad at Carlo for not "helping" her reset her section. Then fellow servers get to enjoy watching Carlo get reamed out for being too slow. By the time poor Carlo even gets back to the dish pit, the news of this fight will get there before he does. The dishwasher looks up and says, "So I hear you and Angie are at it again."

Restaurant relationships cause drama to happen at work, and while your coworkers might love some drama, they get tired of it real quick when it affects their money. If two servers are causing tension among the staff, it affects the mood of the whole restaurant. It puts everyone on edge, and then people are sneaking off around the corner to gossip about the situation instead of doing their jobs.

And let me tell you, even the busiest server will stop dead in his tracks when someone says in a low tone of voice, "Did you hear about Bill and Linda?" No matter how much of a hurry he's in, he'll stop whatever it is he was doing and say, "No, what?" and listen to at least two minutes of relationship crap, ignoring his duties.

Or, even better, let's say you hooked up with a coworker and, for whatever reason, it didn't work out. Then you have to go back to your job and see this person every day. It will be a painful thorn in your side, and it will suck. Don't do it.

If the server couple is happy, it will cause resentment and jealousy and scheduling demands. If the server couple is unhappy, it causes fights at work and drama and wasted time. If the server couple breaks up, one of them will probably do something "sabotogey" to the other one that will affect both of their levels of customer service.

And don't even think about a server/manager romance. Hoo baby! Talk about a loaded situation. Darcy starts sleeping with her manager Fred. Next thing you know, Darcy is always getting the best sections and the easiest side work, and all of her schedule requests are honored. The rest of the staff finds out and is pissed.

They work just as hard as Darcy but aren't getting their fair share of the rewards. Then they start pissing and moaning about it, and it causes disharmony among the staff. Most restaurants absolutely forbid such "fraternization" between management and staff for this very reason and will fire the manager if discovered. So, ol' Fred gets the boot. Then everyone at work is saying, "Did you hear about that *bitch* Darcy? She got Fred fired."

The third type of restaurant romance to be avoided is the server/customer hook-up. Now, a lot of this actually does go on, but it's pretty risky. Let's say you're a cute female bartender. Guys are gonna be flirting with you all night long. The more of a chance they think they have, the better they will tip you. So it's obviously in your own best interest to dress cute, do your hair and makeup, and flirt back if you want to—you'll make more money and the time will pass more quickly.

But at some point, the guy will either ask for your number or give you his. If he asks you to call him, just say "maybe," and leave it at that. If you do call him and end up with him, it will be tough—he'll get jealous of other guys you serve at the bar. After all, he knows what could happen because you did it with him.

Remember, if you hook up with a customer, she knows where you work. She can come in and see you whether you want her to or not, and it can be pretty embarrassing.

If you do really think you've fallen in love with a coworker, manager, or customer, give your two weeks' notice and quit. You'll be better off in the long run—but then again, you will have lost your job, which is why you started working at the restaurant in the first place. So do yourself a favor. Don't make honey where you make your money.

Chapter Thirteen:
The Weeds

"The weeds" is restaurant jargon that every server knows. It refers to a server being in over her head, with too much to do and not enough time to do it. It also means her customers are on the verge of complaining or demanding to get their food/drinks comped. It further means that the server feels desperate.

When a server says "I'm in the weeds," it means he's feeling overwhelmed and is on the edge of a nervous breakdown. This can happen to almost any server when a guest starts demanding too much attention—like, "I'm thinking of ordering the tuna, but I can't decide . . . please describe the entire history of the universe from the beginning so I can make up my mind." The server tries his best to describe it, while his other tables are wondering why he's being so inattentive to them.

Or there's this scenario: A table of ten people all ordered a cappuccino from you, which you have to make by yourself. It takes you two minutes to make one, and you don't have twenty minutes of free time to make them all because another table of four just sat down in your section and they're impatient for you to take their drink order. What do you do? Make the cappuccinos or get the drink order in?

Being in the weeds is a terrible feeling for a server. Your heart is racing, your blood pressure is up, and you feel, well, panicked. The weeds means panic — sheer terror that either the customers are about to hate you or your manager is going to fire you for incompetence.

The weeds means you've lost control of your section of the restaurant and things are going badly. Your customers are angry and unlikely to tip you well. The weeds means you are *fucked*.

But there are ways to get out of the weeds. The first and best way to get out of the weeds is not to get into them in the first place. You manage this by being as prepared as possible, doing everything you can ahead of time. You've already placed all the necessary silverware and plates on the table before the food arrives. You keep the water pitchers filled with lots of ice. If you know you have a large party coming in, you've got an order sheet ready to go to take down their order, with a good pen that works and some back-up pens, as well. You have all the tableware in your section polished and spot-free so no guests will make you exchange them in the middle of a busy night.

Being prepared means you've already memorized the nightly specials, so you don't have to go running off to ask someone but can recite them with poise and confidence. Whatever your guests might want or need, if you can anticipate it, that's one less thing to do, one less burden for you.

The best time to get all of it done is at the beginning of your shift, when opening duties are performed before service begins. A lot of servers will waste this valuable time by standing around, chatting and bitching about life. Let them. You be the self-motivated person who gets his shit done. That way, later on, you'll be ready.

However, even with the utmost preparation, you can still find yourself feeling stressed out and pressured in the middle of a chaotic night. It's how you handle it mentally that separates the men from the boys (or the girls from the women, of course). Being in the weeds is a mental surrender to panic. Don't give into it—get all Jedi on it. Take a deep breath and just focus. Ask yourself, "What is the most important task to take care of at this time?" Do it, and then think of the next most important thing, and so on.

A restaurant manager friend of mine once admitted to me that sometimes, even managers can feel "in the weeds" during hectic evenings, especially when dealing with irate guests behaving with great hostility. His tactic is that he says to himself, "They *can't* eat me." It helps him relax to remember that he *will* be able to walk away from the situation alive.

If you start feeling like you're about to be in the weeds, this is the perfect time to call in all your favors. Hopefully, you will have used your downtime in the past to help out your coworkers. That way, when you really need your friends at work to help you, they will.

With that in mind, here are three steps to help you get out of the weeds:

Step 1: No More Tables.

If your section is not already full, ask the host or manager not to seat you any more tables for at least ten minutes. That's really all the time it takes to get caught up in the restaurant world, and most managers and hosts won't mind holding an unseated table for only ten minutes.

If your section is already full, however, proceed to . . .

Step 2: Get Help Fast.

Find your back-server, bus-boy, or a fellow server and ask him to do one of your tasks for you, like cleaning off a table or refilling drinks. The more quickly you can delegate, the faster you can get your head above water again. Say please. Tell him you'll pay him back or owe him one. My favorite is to ask the coworker for help, and before she can even get a chance to refuse, say, "Oh God, thank you so much! You're a lifesaver!"

Still, sometimes everyone is equally busy, and there's no one who is able to help you. Then, you must proceed to . . .

Step 3: Haul Your Ass.

Step it up a notch and move faster. Don't waste a second talking to anyone if you don't have to. Think, "I'm gonna do this, this, and this," and do whichever task has the most urgent need first. Typically, you can tell by your customers' facial expressions which of them is getting the most impatient. Go to that one first and calm him down. Get him a drink or put in a food order for him. Make sure the table's water glasses are full and there is plenty of bread out for them before you walk away.

And remember this: Smile a lot and speak soothingly to your table. Even if you feel like you're about to lose it, don't let it show in your tone of voice. Your voice should sound calm and peaceful, not hurried and panicked. Talk to your guests in the same tone you would use when trying to talk a baby into going to sleep. Your customers should have no idea that you're stressing inside.

If they can tell you're freaked out, things will get worse quickly. The guests have come to the restaurant to relax, but if they suspect you're losing control, they will assume *they* must now take control of the situation. And that's bad. Your guests are then forced to stop relaxing, do their best to assess the situation, and tell you how to do your job better. They *will* punish you for causing them to stop relaxing.

But they'll reward you if they're able to continue relaxing. So keep your voice very soft and soothing whenever you talk to a customer. Fake it, baby. If a guest snaps, "Why is it taking so long to get our food?" and you secretly know it's because you forgot to input their food order for ten minutes, for God's sake, don't tell them it's all your fault. Simply say with great confidence, "I'm sure your order will be coming right out." Ask if anyone needs a fresh beverage before you walk away.

Eventually, everything will calm down. It always does. Remember that even if you, as a server, screw something up, it's not the end of the world. It's just food and drinks. No one is going to physically die if you forget to ring in a she-crab soup. We're not doing open-heart surgery here, folks. We are simply asking people what they want and then getting it for them.

When things have calmed down again and you're feeling good about all your tables, make sure you take time to verbally thank everyone who helped you during the crush. Tip them out if you can. As a server, you sure as hell hate getting only a verbal tip from your customer. Your coworkers will get real tired real quick if you constantly ask for their help without returning the favor, thanking them, or sharing some of the spoils with them.

The weeds means giving into anxiety. It means the bad guys win. Don't do it—and if you see a fellow server in the weeds, do whatever you can to help her get out of it as fast as possible. That will make everyone's guests have the best possible experience and come back again, and repeat business is the best for everyone.

Chapter Fourteen:
Restaurant Pranks

Note: None of the pranks discussed in this chapter are safe. They could cause damage to property and/or serious bodily injury. None of these pranks should be performed by anyone, ever. To do so could cause loss of life or loss of employment. So don't sue me, bitches. I have expressly told you not *to try this.*

One of my favorite ways to blow off some steam in a restaurant environment is using humor. A good joke or funny story can make you forget all your stress and remove tension. In the restaurant world, besides jokes and funny stories, there's a long tradition of pulling pranks on each other. I'm not exactly sure why—I think it might have something to do with having to kiss the customers' asses so much that you want to be openly mean and cruel to someone on purpose, just to balance it all out. You have to put up with guests being rude and insensitive to you, and you're forced to respond—unnaturally—with sweetness and kindness. Resentment for taking all this crap can build up if you're not careful.

Playing a prank on an unsuspecting coworker can be the perfect way to let off some steam. You have to be careful about it, or you can get in a lot of trouble.

Whatever you choose to do, it can't cause the restaurant to lose any money. It also can't damage any equipment, product, or property. It can't use up a lot of "on-the-clock-time," keep anyone from doing his job, or embarrass a customer. Finally, it can't cause any physical damage to a person—no cuts or burns, please. That's not a prank; it's an attack. All that said, there are still plenty of ways to have a go on your coworkers. Here are some I've seen in action:

The Cinnamon Challenge
In this classic punking, someone on the kitchen staff will tell a rookie server that he can have the biggest steak in the house for free if he'll do just one little thing: swallow a tablespoon of cinnamon. If the server agrees, the cook hands over a soup spoon brimming with ground cinnamon.

"How bad could it be?" thinks the unsuspecting server. "I like cinnamon."

Unfortunately, liking cinnamon doesn't matter. No matter who tries this, the same thing always happens. When you put the spoonful of cinnamon into your mouth, as your lips close around it and your mouth compresses, some of the ground cinnamon shoots up into your sinuses. It burns like hell, and you immediately start sneezing and coughing, with rust-colored smoke clouds flying out of your nostrils and mouth. You look like a dragon. It causes tears, as well.

This is a particularly hateful prank, and I only bring it up to warn you not to fall for it. The back of the house loves to do this to servers, and it takes at least five to ten minutes of splashing yourself in the sink to recover.

Empty the Hot Water
A much more harmless prank is sometimes pulled on someone at the end of her first shift in a restaurant. Almost all restaurant coffee machines have a little hot-water spigot above the coffee pot that's connected to a water line. When pulled, it can produce a never-ending stream of boiling-hot water.

You go over to the newbie and hand him an empty water pitcher. Then you say, "As part of your closing side work, you have to empty out all the hot water from the coffee machine. Fill up the pitcher and dump it out in the sink, and repeat until you get all of it."

I saw one person do this for an hour.

The Old Crazy Phone Conversation
This one works really well if there's a manager within hearing distance. If someone calls on the phone and it's a really quick conversation, and they hang up first, continue talking and have a pretend conversation. Make it as crazy-sounding as possible; say something dirty or suggestive, anything at all, as long as it's one hundred percent inappropriate.

Watch your manager's face as you do this. His eyeballs will pop out, and his jaw will drop. It's awesome. Just make sure the other party is definitely off the line first.

The Fake Broken Dishes Scam
Let's say you have a boss who completely freaks out whenever dishware gets broken—the type of boss who yells out, "Who broke that? I heard that! That's coming out of somebody's paycheck!"

This prank only works if you have a large bin or metal can where all broken dish fragments are tossed. Get a trusted accomplice to help you with this one. Find an empty trash can of approximately equal size to the broken-dishes bin. Get another buddy to act as a lookout to signal you when the manager is within earshot but out of visual range. When the boss is in the ideal area, you and your buddy carefully lift the broken dishes can and tip it over into the empty can. It will sound like every dish in the house is being destroyed at the same time.

Then, run like hell or hide. And remember, you didn't break anything that wasn't already broken in the first place.

When I pulled this one on my Egyptian manager, Mike, he was in the middle of making change for a customer at the cash register. He heard all these glasses smashing and took off running towards the sound, yelling out, "Oh my God! I cannot believe!" He actually left the cash drawer wide open behind him as he sprinted toward the noise. When he got there, he could see what we had done, but we had all run off so as not to be blamed. He roared out, "Dex–torrrrr! I cannot see, but I KNOW IS YOU!!"

Shake It Up
Why limit all your mischief to management? What about getting your fellow servers, as well? The possibilities are endless. Once, I saw a veteran server talking to an especially annoying rookie server. The rookie was asking how to go about opening a bottle of champagne, as he'd never had to do it before.

In great detail, the veteran server perfectly explained the correct way to do it and then added one final bit of instruction: "You want the cork to make a nice loud *pop* when it comes out of the bottle, so make sure you shake up the bottle real good before you open it."

The rookie shook that bottle for a good two minutes and then proceeded to walk over to the table. He delicately removed the foil cap and the little wire cage thingy. Next, as he just barely touched the cork, it exploded out of the bottle and there erupted a fountain of foamy champagne like a geyser. It spewed all over him. The foam literally hit the ceiling. Not a drop was left inside the bottle.

The White Smear
Another server buddy of mine named Roy used to work with me at a hotel restaurant in Indianapolis. All of us servers there would walk around with our server books tucked into our belts at the small of the back. Roy would sneak up behind a fellow server and carefully, but quickly, smear a big glob of sour cream on the server's waiter book. He did this with a feather-light touch that you couldn't feel through the thick vinyl book, and then he would just walk away.

Later on, the victim would walk up to her table, introduce herself, and ask for a drink order. She'd instinctively reach behind her to grab her waiter book to write it down. She'd instantly feel this cold slimy stuff all over her hand, and she was screwed. She couldn't pull her hand back out again, or the guests would see all this white junk all over her hand — that would definitely gross out the table. Instead, she'd just have to kind of stand there the whole time, holding one arm behind her back, feeling and looking like an idiot.

Ye Olde Hot Tea Hater Move

Another waiter-hater server buddy of mine named Dennis used to pull this one on me all the time. Most veteran servers really hate having to make hot tea for a guest—not because they're lazy, but because it truly is a time-consuming pain in the ass. It takes at least five minutes and can really throw off your rhythm on a busy night. So my buddy Dennis used to walk by another server's table as that server was suggesting coffee and dessert, and he would just shout out, "Hot tea for anyone?" with a big smile on his face. Sometimes, he would even go so far as to drop off a whole assortment of tea bags on the table as well. Bastard.

Frozen Solid

Jason, my back of the house buddy in Roanoke, Virginia, is very fond of freezing people's keys or cell phone (wrapped in a Ziploc bag) in a ginormous block of ice. To accomplish this, he finds the biggest pan he can. He fills it halfway with water and places it on a shelf in the walk-in freezer. After a couple hours, when the pan is frozen solid, he places the victim's belongings on top of the ice and completely fills the pan with water, which freezes again, leaving the personal item trapped at the dead center of a concrete-hard, foot-high ice block.

At the end of the shift, the encased item is placed on a counter for all to see. It takes at least a twenty minutes of careful chipping to get to its center without harming the contents—*so* not fun when all the victim had wanted to do was get the hell out of the restaurant as fast as possible at the end of his shift.

Have fun with that one, kiddies.

A Glass of Pain

I've also witnessed many an unsuspecting server having his own personal beverage tampered with. A fellow server sneaks a few drops of hot sauce into the other server's drink, and then, when the poor server comes by later and swallows a big old swig of it, he's treated to liquid fire.

I personally find this so-called prank to be particularly *un*funny and extremely douchey. A server only has a few seconds to down a beverage on a busy night, if he is lucky. All the staff members running around in a restaurant need to stay hydrated, and sometimes they won't have time to dump out a contaminated drink and get a fresh one. Plus, this particular "prank" has a way of escalating, as the first server invariably takes revenge later.

Eventually, the whole staff has to start taking a baby sip of their drink first to make sure it hasn't been compromised. So don't pull this prank, and don't allow your coworkers to, either.

High Times

However, a truly funny one to pull is tricking a fellow server into thinking she's found a small amount of drugs, like a "dime bag" of weed or cocaine. All you need for this prank is a tiny piece of plastic wrap and a teaspoon of either powdered sugar/flour or any cooking herb, fresh or dried, as long as it's green. You put it in the center of a two-inch square of plastic wrap, and then carefully wrap the plastic tightly around it and twist it all up into one little point. Voila! You've got a fake drug bag that looks like it contains the real thing. Place this decoy somewhere in a service area where only a fellow employee can find it, and hide yourself within visual range.

Make sure you can peek and see who grabs it up. This is an awesome way to find out how many hard-core druggies you have on staff. (As if you didn't know already . . .) I once saw my buddy Shane snatch for the baggie so quickly that his arm looked like a cobra striking its prey. It's even more entertaining if you have another coworker watching with you, so you can share the laugh.

Big Earner
This next prank is tailor-made for that fellow server who's always bragging about how big his tips are. It appeals to his sense of jealousy in a very gratifying fashion. As I'm sure you already know, when customers pay by credit card, they always receive two credit card slips — one for them, and one for the restaurant.

These days, customers will often only fill out and sign one slip and leave an additional, completely blank, credit slip behind.

Here's what you do: Go ahead and close out the signed credit slip with the check, with the actual legal amount, in the service computer and put it away with the rest of your closed checks. Next, get the blank credit slip and fill in some outrageous tip, like one hundred bucks on a thirty-five-dollar check. Total it, and scribble on the signature line.

Next, place the receipt, along with a pen, in a check presenter somewhere that the most envious or arrogant coworker will find it. Naturally, he'll open it up and get royally pissed that you scored this amazing tip and he didn't.

When he confronts you about it, just say something like, "Oh, really? I'm not surprised—they told me I gave them the best service they've ever had." Then smile, take the fake credit slip, and walk away quietly. Go around a corner, tear it up, and discreetly throw it in the trash. This one really burns up a jealous coworker.

Wild Goose Chase

I've also seen the kitchen staff pull some fast ones on the front of the house staff, especially on rookies. For example, a cook will tell a newbie to go get something that plain doesn't exist, like, "Go upstairs into the dry storage area where we keep the extra kitchen utensils and bring back the bacon-stretcher." (Because, of course, the bacon gets all nervous and tense and needs to be stretched back out flat again.) So the server wanders around the dry storage area for five minutes, scratching her head with a confused look on her face. Eventually, a coworker or manager will ask her what she's looking for, and she says she's trying to find the bacon-stretcher. The coworker starts laughing and the newbie realizes she's been had. Then she has to walk back to the kitchen all red-faced and be greeted with howling laughter from all the cooks, feeling like a complete dumbass and wondering why the kitchen hates her.

Pootamoo Sauce

A related prank I've often seen the kitchen staff pull on a server is to tell the rookie to walk across the street to a nearby restaurant and ask to borrow something.

There are times that this can indeed be a legitimate task—I've been sent to bring back things like cocktail napkins, straws, or even lemons, with the understanding that my restaurant would return the items when our next shipment arrived. But this is different.

I have seen rookie servers sent out to ask for things that plain don't exist, like, "Hey, I work for the restaurant across the street, and my boss wants to know if you can loan us a little 'poo-ta-moo' sauce."

Of course, the other restaurant staff is all, "What the hell is pootamoo sauce?"

The rookie has to admit that he has no idea what pootamoo sauce is, and that he was simply told to go out and borrow some. Sometimes, the rookie will actually keep going from restaurant to restaurant, repeatedly asking to borrow some pootamoo sauce in an attempt to not come back empty-handed. The harder he keeps trying to acquire it, the funnier it is for the kitchen staff when the poor sucker comes back and admits defeat. And of course, all this is done just to embarrass the poor kid.

Restaurant pranks are part of the whole food and beverage culture. If one happens to you, take it in stride and laugh. If you get mad, it only tells the rest of the staff that you're a jerk; that's what all these pranks really are—a test to see who is cool and who isn't.

Chapter Fifteen:
The Dark Side of Waiting Tables

In every profession, there's a downside, and that's definitely true for serving. I've already discussed the dangers of "losing it" due to over-exposure to constant guest demands. I have also talked about the mental trap of falling "in the weeds." But don't worry — there is plenty more negativity to watch out for in the food and beverage industry.

Because of the high employee turnover rate in restaurants, several types of scam artists can easily infiltrate the staff, at least for a short time. These scammers are attracted to the business because of the promise of quick money and the anonymity that serving provides. The following are just a few shady things I've witnessed firsthand.

I worked at a major four-star steakhouse with a server named Keith. This guy was so shady that whenever he got a table with a toddler, he would ask the parents if they would like their little one to have the "child lobster dinner." Usually, the father didn't want to ask out loud how much it would cost, for fear of looking cheap. After all, how much could a kid's meal cost, anyway?

When the parents said yes, Keith would walk over to the lobster tank and fish out one of the smaller lobsters, say a two-pounder, which still cost sixty bucks. The unsuspecting customers had no idea that the "child lobster dinner" was going to cost more than ten dollars. When they got the check, most of the time they were too embarrassed to dispute the bill, and they just ate it.

Some of our restaurant's regional managers would praise his salesmanship because they never had to witness the angry parents stomping out of the restaurant, never to return again. This guy Keith couldn't have cared less. Even if the family only left him a ten percent tip, he still made twice what he would have made if the toddler had just eaten off a parent's plate.

I have also seen some servers take advantage of corporate pharmaceutical banquet dinners. Usually, the pharmaceutical representative who's hosting the dinner is very busy setting up audio/visual equipment, greeting the speaker, and welcoming all the attendees.

At the end of the meal, there's a mad rush for all of the doctors and nurses to be signed up for some type of product or service. This is the perfect time for an unscrupulous server to start padding the bill. I've seen servers ring in steaks for themselves to take home in to-go boxes, or send drink tickets to the bar to be made for them to consume secretly. I have often observed servers opening up multiple bottles of wine for a banquet ahead of time, with the alleged purpose of saving time later. The server gets to charge the pharmaceutical company for each bottle of wine that was opened, even if not one sip of the wine inside was consumed. She gets an additional automatic gratuity on that bottle of wine, and oftentimes will take the bottle home to be consumed later at her leisure.

I once worked an incredibly fancy, expensive wedding banquet. The father of the bride wanted all two hundred guests to drink Vueve Clicquot champagne after the cake was cut. We ran out of Vueve Clicquot less than halfway through pouring for all the attendees.

In a private service area, my manager had us secretly pour a super-cheap house champagne into the pretty — but empty — gold Veuve Clicquot bottles and then go out onto the banquet floor and act as if we were pouring the good stuff. And yes, the father of the bride did get charged more than seventy dollars apiece for every three-dollar bottle we poured. I'm not particularly proud of that moment in my food service career.

One of the dumbest ways a server can try to scam is to alter the guest's credit card receipt to change the total and increase his tip. I have seen so many servers get fired for this one. I really don't know why these servers thought the guests would never notice. These days, folks are watching every penny they have and checking their online balance constantly.

Another aspect of the dark side of waiting tables is the vicious cycle of working and then over-partying night after night. Here is a brief example of what can happen to a server if he's not careful: The whole crew wants to go party for any particular reason—could be someone's going-away party, new apartment party, anything.

The party is hilarious, and everyone is doing too many shots, too much smoking/drugging, and pretty much acting like Prohibition is about to start up again at dawn. Somehow, the server makes it home or finds somewhere to crash for the night. The next day (or afternoon), the crusty-faced food service employee looks at the clock and says the word "fuck" three times really fast. Maybe there's time for a quick shower before the next shift begins, or maybe he's already late and will only have time for a quick wash and wipe. So he barely makes it into work on time, having eaten nothing beforehand, and possibly being in the same work clothes he'd had on during his last shift.

During the whole shift, the server is alternating between hating himself and praying for death. I've found that there's an inverse proportion or Murphy's Law stating that the more unprepared a server is for a busy shift, the busier it will be.

Even if the server feels like complete crap all during meal service, he's still likely to make money. By the end of the shift, the adrenaline has carried the server all the way through, and he can't believe he fooled everyone and got away with it with cash in hand. It seems too good to be true. The server looks at the rest of the staff and says, "So, what's everybody doing tonight?" and the whole cycle begins again. Rinse and repeat for the next five to ten years, and the server has become trapped in what I like to call the "Perpetual Frat-Boy Lifestyle."

This problem can be further reinforced because of the late-night hours most servers work. Odds are you aren't going to meet a lot of church-going folk at the bar after two a.m. Therefore, most of your coworkers and bar buddies are going to tell you how awesome you are, and how good a server you are, and all that kind of crap. "These people get me," you think. "I have finally found my niche where I'm accepted and appreciated."

Whether or not you're truly awesome is none of my business, but when all your work buddies have a good buzz on, they'll tell you all kinds of good, glowing stuff. Just remember, the majority of the nine-to-five crowd thinks of servers as only slightly less grifty than carnies.

If you lose touch with all your friends and family in the first-shift world, you can lose a very valuable perspective. Servers can end up living in the shadowy world of the evening. Make sure you always leave a little room for the light of day and those who live within it.

Chapter Sixteen:
The Ultimate Tip

Writing this book has been a lot of fun for me. It has caused me to really think about what I do at my restaurant every night. So many of the things I say and do each night are things I've done over and over again, thousands and thousands of times. I take it for granted, I guess. It's now nearly effortless for me to take care of each table in such a way as to make the maximum tip at each one.

That said, I didn't want to finish this book with me tooting my own horn. I've struggled in deciding what I wanted to leave you with at the end of this book, but I think I finally figured out what I'd like to give you the most—besides upgrading your skill level and teaching you how to beat the system.

I want to share with you what still keeps me going after twenty-five years in the great food service army.

To be a server means that you're in the business of serving others. Service, however, is something far deeper than that. True service can only be achieved by an individual with a passion to be his or her best. It means doing more than just phoning it in and barely getting through each shift. It's a commitment to doing your job at the highest level you're capable of every time.

True service comes from a genuine desire to help others. If you honestly don't like other people, get out of the restaurant game as fast as you can. Your customers can tell.

Service is more than just handling plates and glasses all night. It's an art form, like ballet. It can comfort other human beings and turn their whole day around. You can make your guests feel like they are more than just consumers. You can let them know that you're aware they are *people*.

And you can take great pride in this. Don't ever let anyone make you feel you're subservient to them because you are serving them. You are not a slave; you voluntarily accepted the job. So kick ass at it.

Knowing that you're awesome at your job will give you both confidence and poise. You don't have to feel like you're a loser because you wait tables. Anyone who can hold down a job as stressful as working in a restaurant deserves mad street cred. Hold your head up high as you greet each customer.

So what keeps me going? I have a lot of fun at work–a *lot* of fun. More fun, I think, than most other people have every day at their jobs. I go into a really cool, hip environment, work with all these young, sexy people, serve awesome food, and get paid well to do it.

In addition, I make a difference in other people's lives. When I'm waiting on guests who are celebrating their anniversary, I like to make it as special as possible for them. I give them every little extra special touch I can. I try to be unobtrusive and respond as silently as I can so that all the focus is on them. I know it's really working when they stop talking and just hold hands while they look in each other's eyes.

There are times I'll be waiting on someone who is having a bad day. It's like they're in a dark hole in their own mind and can barely see me at the top. Throughout the course of the meal, my kindness and attentiveness can make them want to crawl out of that hole and rejoin humanity. They walked in the restaurant grouchy and growling, and left with a grin on their face. Sometimes, they even make sure to wave at me and call me by name as they walk out the door. It makes me feel good.

I have some regular customers who used to have a reputation for being nasty and demanding. The first time I had to wait on them, I was repeatedly warned by my fellow servers to watch out. I found that it wasn't that they were mean people at all. It's just that they're extremely specific about how they like their drinks to be prepared and their food served. Apparently, in the past, my fellow servers always managed to disappoint these very discriminating guests.

I didn't. By the end of their meal, they had seemed to relax a little bit. For once, they had gotten everything they wanted just the way they wanted it. They spent a lot of money and left me a very nice tip. That was a couple years ago. These days, if they walk into the restaurant and I'm not there, they turn around and head back out. They aren't rude about it. They just want to have a server who cares enough to pay attention. There are some benefits to always bringing your "A" game.

You know what else keeps me going? Messing with my coworkers' heads all the time. I am notorious at my restaurant for my twisted sense of humor.

I love to whisper something outrageously inappropriate to a coworker while he's dealing with a guest, or make faces at a server who is talking to a table (where the guests can't see me, of course). Or I pretend to be insane in front of a newbie. That one never gets old.

Another unexpected side effect of working with a staff that's perpetually in their early twenties is the perspective it offers. I'm always treated to the current mindset of the youth culture, which changes dramatically and quite quickly. I'm always up to date on trends, movies, songs, and the slang of the very young. Keeps me in the loop, so to speak—which is ironic, actually. When I started out in the food service army, I was the youngest kid in the room. Nowadays, if I'm not the oldest person on the schedule for that night, I'm like, "Boooyahh!"

Remember this above all else: Every night you go into work, make sure you have as much fun as possible. I don't care if the restaurant is so slammed that you're completely stressed out. In the heat of battle, amidst the chaos, take a moment to see the humor in it all.

It could be the last night of your life. None of us has one more moment promised to us. So even if you're working in the middle of the busiest shift ever, try to enjoy every second of this amazing thing called your *life* as richly as possible. That's my ultimate tip.

Glossary of Restaurant Terminology

- **86**: To be out of stock. Example: "The tuna entree has been 86ed."

- **All day**: A readjusted verbal count tally of a particular food/drink item that needs to be prepared, meaning 'altogether.' Example: "You were waiting on three orders of fries and now you're waiting for two more, so that's five orders all day."

- **Auction it off**: The embarrassing task of having to verbally interrupt a table as food is served because the server can't figure out the pre-assigned seat numbers, causing the server to have to ask where each dish needs to go, as in "Who got the swordfish?" Example: "You rang in your table seat numbers wrong and we had to auction it off!"

- **Auto-grat**: An automatic gratuity added to a guest's check, usually because of large party size. Usually, it's twenty percent of the total bill. Example: "I need the manager to put the auto-grat on table thirteen."

- **A walk-in**: A guest who has arrived at the restaurant without a reservation. Example: "Guys, the restaurant is completely booked up tonight, so no walk-ins."

- **Back of the house**: The restaurant staff that usually has no direct contact with the paying guests and yet does most of the hard work for less pay than the front of the house employees, including food preparation and dishwashing.

- **Call liquor**: Medium-priced liquors that cost more than well brands but less than top-shelf ones.

- **Campers**: Restaurant guests who remain seated at a table long after the bill has been paid, resulting in the server's inability to reseat the table with new guests and generate more money from it. Example: "Oh God, don't put the Schmidts in my section! They're such campers!"

- **Closer**: The server assigned to stay the latest, take the last guests, and ensure all required closing side work has been done correctly. Example: "Don't piss me off, honey. I'm the closer, and I won't sign you out."

- **Cut**: When a manager decides to send a server home early either due to lack of business or the server's inappropriate attitude/behavior. Example: "Gosh, it's so slow in here tonight. Hope I get cut."

- **Double grat**: When a guest either knowingly or unknowingly adds an additional tip on top an automatic gratuity that was previously added. Example: "Woo-hoo! I just made two hundred bucks on a double grat!"

- **Double seat**: A situation in which a server has two different tables sit down at exactly the same time in his section, resulting in one table having to wait while the server is busy greeting the other table. Example: "Hey, can you greet table sixteen for me? I just got double seated."

- **Dragging item**: Part of a food/drink order that has yet to be completed, even though everything else is ready and waiting to be delivered. Example: "Go ahead and take your table's food out to them. You're dragging fries, but we'll send them right out."

- **Dying in the window**: Restaurant dishes that have been cooked correctly and are sitting under the heat lamps. They're starting to dry out because they cannot be immediately delivered to the table, either because the rest of the order is incomplete, or no will deliver it. This results in the food drying out and losing its visual appeal. Example: "Hurry up and run this food out! It's dying in the window!"

- **Fire**: A verbal instruction by the chef to the cooks to begin the preparation of a table's next course. Example: "Fire table ten's salads!"

- **Fired**: Food that has already started to be prepared. Example: "Make sure your table has the correct silverware once their order has been fired."

- **Food cost**: The percentage of money required to pay for all of the wholesale food product ordered by the chef. Example: "Every time you servers drop a hot plate because you didn't use a napkin, you completely fuck my food cost!"

- **Front of the house**: All of the restaurant staff who has direct contact with the guests, including hosts, bussers, bartenders, servers, and management. Example: "We have a front of the house meeting this Saturday, guys."

- **House/rail/well liquor**: The cheapest brand of liquor in the restaurant, which will automatically be used to make a cocktail if a more expensive type of liquor isn't requested. Example: "What's your house vodka?" "It's Popov." "Oh, hell no! Give me Grey Goose instead!"

- **In the weeds**: A state of panic experienced by a server who cannot meet the demands placed upon her, usually caused either by inexperience or high volume within the restaurant. Example: "Don't give me another table for at least fifteen minutes. I'm in the weeds!"

- **Kitchen crashed**: A very unpleasant situation that is caused when the back of the house can't keep up with all of the food orders coming in and get completely overwhelmed. This results in outrageously long cooking times for each ticket. Example: "It took an hour for me to get two Caesar salads because the kitchen crashed!"

- **Line up**: The daily meeting between the front of the house and the back of the house to discuss menu changes, specials, and 86ed items—and to bitch out incompetent servers. Also sometimes known as the server meeting. Example: "Guys, line up is in five minutes, so don't be late!"

- **Liquor cost**: The percentage of money required to wholesale purchase all the beer, wine, and liquor before it's marked up for the guest. Example: "Our liquor cost is through the roof! You guys are either overpouring or stealing—or both!"

- **MOD**: The manager on duty, who is above all other assistant managers. Example: "I hate it when Brad is MOD. He's such an asshole."

- **Repeat**: A returning restaurant guest. Example: "You just pissed off table fourteen, and they were repeats!"

- **Rezzo**: Abbreviated form of "reservation." Opposite of a walk-in. Example: "How many rezzos we got tonight?"

- **Seat number**: A preassigned delegation of numbered seats at each table in the restaurant so that food can be delivered correctly. Also known as pivot points. Example: "Hey, I don't know who gets the shrimp cocktail on table six. What's the seat number?"

- **Side work**: The untipped duties a server is required to perform before, during, and after each shift, such as glass polishing, cleaning, and bathroom checks. Example: "I quit my last restaurant because of all the side work."

- **Skate**: To leave the restaurant at the end of the shift before having done the allocated share of the closing side work, resulting in the designated closer getting stuck having to do it. Example: "You guys skated out of here last night and left me with six racks of glasses to polish!"

- **Stiff**: For a guest to pay only for the amount of the check and leave no gratuity for the server. Example: "That cheap bitch stiffed me!"

- **Ticket time**: How long it takes for the kitchen staff to prepare the necessary food items required to complete the order. This is calculated by subtracting the printed-out time on the order ticket and subtracting it from the current time. Example: "It's taking forever to get my table's appetizers!" "Hey, I just checked the ticket time, and it's only been eight minutes. So you can fuck off!"

- **Tip out**: The percentage of money a server is forced by management to take from his nightly earned gratuities and share with his back-servers and bartenders. Example: "I made a hundred bucks tonight but had to tip out thirty-seven."

- **Tip pool, or pool tips**: When a group of servers either willingly or unwillingly places all of their individual gratuities into one pile and distributes them equally among all. Example: "I hate to pool tips with Bev. She's sooooo lazy."

- **Top-shelf liquors**: The most expensive brand of each type of liquor, usually prominently displayed up high on the bar liquor shelves. Example: "Gimme a top-shelf margarita with salt."

- **Turn time**: The amount of time it takes to get a table to sit down, order, dine, pay, and leave so that the table can be reset to accommodate the next waiting guests. Example: "You guys have to have quicker turn times so we can get all these rezzos in on time."

- **Two-top, three-top, four-top**: A table of two, three, or four. Instead of saying "a table of four," it is merely referred to as a "four-top." Example: "I just sat a six-top in your section, so go eat a mint before you go over there with your cigarette breath."

- **Upsell**: To persuade a guest to order a more expensive item than they were initially willing to. For instance, if a guest orders a rum and Coke, the bartender can say, "You want Bacardi?" to get the guest to purchase a call brand of liquor, which is more expensive than the house liquor. Example: "You guys need to quit ringing in house liquors and upsell the top-shelf brands."

- **Verbal grat**: Abbreviated form of "verbal gratuity." This is the dreaded practice of a table telling their server how much they appreciated him and then proceeding to leave a terrible tip. Example: "Table twelve only left me two bucks. Guess I got the verbal grat."

- **Walking in**: A verbal call the chef makes as food orders print out in the kitchen, letting the cooks know what new items need to be started. Example: "Walking in . . . three chicken parmesans and one fettuccine alfredo."

- **The walk-in**: A large walk-in refrigeration area where all the food that must be kept cool is stored. Example: "I just checked the walk-in, and we are out of half-and-half."

- **Walk-out**: A table that prematurely leaves the restaurant because of extreme dissatisfaction, usually caused by excessive ticket times or poor service. Example: "Thanks to a forty-five-minute ticket time, table seven was a walk-out!"

www.ingramcontent.com/pod-product-compliance
Lightning Source LLC
Chambersburg PA
CBHW021820170526
45157CB00007B/2659